Self Love 101

Also by this author . . . .

God in a Black Jag Blue Pearl Press 1998

Self Love 101

A Gentle Guide to Loving Your Self
Unconditionally and Fulfilling
Your Life Purpose

Timothy Ernster

BALBOA.
PRESS
A DIVISION OF HAY HOUSE

Balboa Press books may be ordered through booksellers or by contacting:

Balboa Press
A Division of Hay House
1663 Liberty Drive
Bloomington, IN 47403
www.balboapress.com
1-(877) 407-4847

Because of the dynamic nature of the Internet, any web addresses or
links contained in this book may have changed since publication and
may no longer be valid. The views expressed in this work are solely those
of the author and do not necessarily reflect the views of the publisher,
and the publisher hereby disclaims any responsibility for them.

The author of this book does not dispense medical advice or prescribe the use
of any technique as a form of treatment for physical, emotional, or medical
problems without the advice of a physician, either directly or indirectly. The
intent of the author is only to offer information of a general nature to help
you in your quest for emotional and spiritual well-being. In the event you use
any of the information in this book for yourself, which is your constitutional
right, the author and the publisher assume no responsibility for your actions.

Any people depicted in stock imagery provided by Thinkstock are models,
and such images are being used for illustrative purposes only.
Certain stock imagery © Thinkstock.

Printed in the United States of America.

ISBN: 978-1-4525-7958-0 (sc)
ISBN: 978-1-4525-7960-3 (hc)
ISBN: 978-1-4525-7959-7 (e)

Library of Congress Control Number: 2013914292

Balboa Press rev. date: 2/26/2014

Table of Contents

With Gratitude

Special thanks to Marla Owens for her constant love and support, for always being there for the highs, the lows, and everything in between, for loving unconditionally. I also wish to thank Marie Lise Labonte for all that I have gained through knowing her and for holding a higher vision of me even when I myself had lost sight of it. My thanks to Alan Dolan for "the breath" and for his input into the creation of this book. My heartfelt thanks to Gina Zuliani for her love and support throughout the years. My thanks to my family, my friends, my teachers, my students, and to all those that I have been blessed to encounter on this amazing journey. And to you, my imagined unseen audience, for you have drawn these words, this book, from deep within me. Thank you. Finally, I offer my deep gratitude to my spiritual Master whose unconditional love I strive to emulate and whose enlightened wisdom has guided me moment by moment on my path of self love.

Introduction

"What is my life's purpose? How can I grow to love myself unconditionally? Will I ever know true peace?"

The answer to the first question lies within the second. After 30 years of studying with Enlightened Masters and traveling my own life path, I have come to the conclusion that the primary purpose in life *is* to come to love ourselves unconditionally and, in doing so, rediscover the abiding peace within us. In this book, **SELF LOVE 101,** I draw upon the ancient wisdom that I was given by the Masters with whom I studied and upon my own uncommon life experiences to guide you on this simple path of self-love. What is it that keeps you from loving yourself unconditionally? How do you address the issues, the self-judgments, the deep wounds that separate you from this love? With loving compassion, I will introduce you to yourself. Before you can love yourself you must first truly know yourself. I provide the tools for you to do so. I share with you my own powerful experiences on the path of love. You will discover that the teachers that you require are all around you, that your life provides you with opportunities to know yourself and find love there. I will guide you into becoming the master of your own life, to manifest the realization of your dreams, to reclaim your peace. I offer you the tools and teachings that worked for me. They are proven. They work. These are the basics. **SELF LOVE 101**. These are the principles supporting my path, the path of self-love. It can also be your path. Unconditional love awaits you. Peace awaits you. It is time to begin.

This guide, this book, is short in length and long in content. I encourage you to take your time with it. Read a chapter. Reflect. Practice. Read again. It is presented somewhat as a beginner's manual, a basic course. Contained within these pages are the essentials. I have intentionally kept it as simple as possible. If you are already deeply immersed in your conscious journey toward unconditional love of self, it is still well worth reading. Timely reminders to provoke an expansion, to make more clear the way home. It has certainly been that for me in the writing of it.

CHAPTER I

Loving My Self

I LOVE MY SELF. Me, with all my flaws and imperfections, my gifts, my talents, my reticence, my exuberance, my procrastinations, my kindness, my laziness, my passions, my insecurities, my sense of humor, my compassion, what society would call my failures, my successes, what I deem to be my beauty and the lack thereof. I LOVE ME!!!

I KNOW MY SELF I have spent many years getting to know me, to know myself, looking deeply into the dark corridors of the house that is ME. I have looked. I have judged. I have despised some of what I saw. From some corridors I have run screaming in denial. "No. That is not me!" In humility I have returned again and again until I could find acceptance and with acceptance, forgiveness. I have been guided on my journey by wise and all-loving Masters, by angels in my corner, and by those who have walked beside me—friends, fellow disciples, family, teachers, and students. I have been guided and I have done the work. Overcoming skepticism and stubbornness I have been willing to look. I wanted to know—to know myself. I wanted to know and to love ME. Myself. As I AM. Wholly and unconditionally.

That, I now see, has been my path. Until now, I have called it a spiritual path and it has been that for certain. But what does that mean finally, a spiritual path? The mystics call it a path to enlightenment but enlightenment is so difficult to define and seems so far beyond who I am and what I can be. But Self Love? That I can grasp. And I can see that this has been my path all along, no matter what it looked like at the time. Building a successful manufacturing business. Chanting and meditating with my Master at his ashram. Becoming the devoted disciple. Exploring my sexuality. Traveling the world. Guiding others into a transcendent state. Sharing the wisdom I have gained. Living quietly with family and friends. The common thread through it all? Seeking to know myself and love myself unconditionally.

This is my path—the path of self love. This is the purpose of my life. This, too, can be your path. You have come here to know and love yourself unconditionally. You may choose not to. You are free. You may already be striding passionately down this path. Good for you. You may perhaps see the path ahead of you but are hesitant to begin. I understand. The purpose of this book is to share with you what I have learned, what has worked for me in attaining greater love of self. Offered here are insights, tools, techniques and personal stories to inspire and exemplify. This is **SELF LOVE 101**, a basic course in self-mastery.

My story. Who am I? We shall begin with "I was born . . . .". In Texas. Upper middle class Catholic family. An easy, fairly normal, small town growing up experience. University degree in business. I entered the family business after college and with my dad started a door manufacturing company which by the 1980's had become the most successful in the US. In the midst of my success and material wealth I had a life-changing experience. Introduced unexpectedly to an extraordinary master teacher, I was, despite great skepticism, swept into a journey into self-awareness, into loving the self. I was, quite simply, thunderstruck. I had had no idea that up to this point I really did not know ME, did not know what I felt, what I really believed. Despite my worldly success I was riddled with self-doubt and self-judgment, especially regarding my sexuality. Although I was exploring my homosexuality I kept it very hidden from most of the people around me. I was driven in all aspects of my life by a deep desire to be loved—by my family, my friends, my employees, my peers, my lovers, my teachers. By God. I did not have a clue that what I was really driven by was the desire to be loved by me. Not a clue. Not then. Not for a long time.

My studies with this amazing teacher opened the doorway into myself. I began to see myself more clearly and love myself more easily. It was a beginning. A few years into my studies I was introduced to another teacher who became my Spiritual Master. After a time his work took on the qualities of a spiritual path very much in the Eastern tradition. Meditation, chant, yoga, devotional work, prayer, and always, always, the revelation of oneself to oneself. In his approach everything that we are (even those dark corridors that we despise and judge) is good enough to be loved. In his vernacular, "Everything is God. Everything is good enough to be God. To be loved". It was his job, and ours, to expose those dark corridors and find forgiveness for self. He did so relentlessly and with great love and compassion. We did so, haltingly, begrudgingly, steadily. It was a journey both illuminating and exhausting. We created an ashram in the mountains of Oregon to which many of us retreated from our lives out in the world to live and work and study together. This Master is, in my experience, truly enlightened. Unconditional love radiates from his being. He sees and knows everything.

When you look into his eyes you know, in that moment, that you are loved and that you are worth loving.

In 1994, when I left the ashram, I wrote a book about these awakening experiences and my journey with these two Masters. It is titled GOD IN A BLACK JAG. If you want to know more about this phase of my own path you can find it on my website: www.timothyernster.com.

Little did I know that when I left the Master's presence my journey would truly begin. I had been given the wisdom and the tools. Now I would be pressed to apply them. On my own. Alone in the world. Twenty years have passed. I have accomplished much but I am still a work in progress. Since leaving the ashram I have traveled promoting the book and have given seminars on awakening to our own Christ Consciousness. I have led guided meditations for healing and transformation, and counseled many on their own life issues and challenges on their personal paths to loving themselves more completely. I have been the channel of grace that allowed healings to occur. I worked for a number of years with my good friend, Marie Lise Labonte, who is a successful author, channel, and teacher in the field of self-healing and personal transformation and founder of the Method MLC. She introduced me to the French speaking communities in Quebec and Europe with whom I found for myself a spiritual home and an audience for my work.

Eight years ago I returned home to Texas, called by a desire to be closer to my aging parents and my family and to establish roots again after many years of living as a spiritual gypsy. I stopped teaching and became a realtor. I quietly maintained my spiritual practices and continued to walk the path that I now define as the path of self love. I became private rather than public on my path. A year ago, while on a trip of self-exploration to Italy and France, I began to reflect upon my life from the standpoint of 64 years well-lived. In reflecting, I began to write, to share my reflections, and to define more clearly this path that I now see that I have been on for all of these 64 years. This book was birthed from those reflections. It has served me in gaining clarity and expanded my wisdom and understanding. It is my prayer that it can also serve you. Welcome to **SELF LOVE 101.**

Through my own journey I have come to realize that, finally, the path toward enlightenment that we hear and read so much about is much more about gaining self-knowledge and self-love than it is about any particular form of worship or spiritual practices. The means to gain that knowledge and love is at your fingertips. The world around you will always reflect to you what you need to see about yourself—that aspect of yourself that you do not accept, that you do not love, that you judge. You need only the desire to know and the willingness to look. Once you make a personal decision, a true commitment to know yourself and love yourself, the Universe will supply you with all the teachers and mirrors that you require. Yes, you need also to seek out wisdom so that you can understand what you are seeing and so that you have tools with which to reconcile. The wisdom is out there. The tools are many. "Ask and you shall receive."

In that you have read this far I am going to assume that you are also at a place in your life of reflecting upon your life, of questioning:

"Why with all that I have, I have not peace?
Why with all those around me who love me do I not
feel loved?
What is my purpose in life?
Why am I here?"

Yes, those questions and many more. Good. I am going to continue then to share with you what I have learned, the answers I have received through the life I have lived and the wisdom I have gained. I know that by sharing with you I will gain even greater clarity and receive refined understandings of the answers to my own similar questions. My masters and teachers gave me great and ancient teachings, truths that have stood the test of time. Such wisdom that I now own arrived long after the receipt of the teachings, came only through the attempt to live what I had been given, through ardent application, with patience and compassion for myself.

To have had the opportunity to study with an Enlightened Master gives one an advantage for sure. Nothing else in my own life can begin to compare to that experience. I have been blessed beyond measure. There is no greater evocation of self-love than gazing into the Master's eyes and seeing only love, unconditional and eternal, reflected back to you. No judgment. To understand that the Master sees all, knows all of your "dirty" secrets, and still there is only love. Such a reflection is precious and priceless. And yet it is also only the beginning, a taste of what is true, of what is possible. It allows you to feel in that moment that you are indeed worth loving unconditionally. You do not know it yet but you can at least begin to believe in the possibility. To know it you must look openly and honestly at all of the aspects of yourself that you judge to be unworthy of love. As I said before, if you do not have a Master to expose you to yourself, the world around you will do so—unfailingly. The classroom of Self Love 101? You are already in it.

It begins with those closest to you—your family, lovers, close friends, co-workers. They are your mirrors. They will reveal you to yourself. They become your teachers. Life, your life, becomes your teacher. The signs and messages will appear. You must have the willingness and the awareness to notice them.

I quote from one of Paulo Coelho's inspiring books, "The Zahir":

"All you have to do is to pay attention; lessons always arrive when you are ready, and if you can read the signs, you will learn everything you need to know in order to take the next step."

And so, although I left the outward work of personal transformation (studying with teachers, teaching others) when I returned to Texas, I did not quit the process of growth toward greater self-love. Indeed, I returned to the core issues revolving around family—parents and siblings—still unresolved and begging to be healed. They became my classroom, my ashram, the school of my self-awareness. The stronger aspects of our conditioning are born there with those with whom we grew up, those who first influenced our feelings of self-worth and self-love, those who first taught us who we need to be, how we needed to behave, in order to be loved. At a time when we are the most vulnerable, these conditions penetrate our soul and consciousness, our mind and body. The rules are established.

"I will love you if . . . .". This we call conditioning. From there it continues in the classroom, through the media, in churches, temples, and synagogues, in the work place, and in our cultural environment. But the beginning is in the family and these are the most firmly rooted conditions. I had conquered many but obviously not all.

Being dedicated to the process, I therefore found myself called home to complete the healing, to find greater unconditional love of myself where the conditional was first impressed upon me, to explore the nuances, the subtleties, looking into the mirrors called mother, dad, brother, sister. It has not been a painful or difficult look. I have done a lot of work on myself over the past 25 years. It has been more of an easing into loving acceptance, of being at peace with that which they reflect to me; accepting "them" with love more unconditional, well aware that in so doing I am accepting the part of me that they reflect or represent. It has been an internal process. They are not even aware that it is happening. We are simply living our lives in close proximity. There is no need to discuss the "issues". They are *my* issues, *my* reflections. It is not about them and certainly not about changing them. It is about me—mining those final nuggets of gold called "that which I do not love of myself". It has been a beautiful experience mostly although not always easy. And after eight years, I feel that the work is nearly done. Now I am ready to teach again, to share with others like you what I have learned on this life-long journey, this path, the Path of Love of Self.

CHAPTER II

Life Purpose

This book was birthed from a contemplation on life from the vantage point of sixty some accumulated years well lived. That contemplation reflects the spiritual wisdom gained, the wisdom of a deeply explored self. It also reflects the influence of travel and the exploration of other cultures, lifestyles, religions. I share the fruits of that contemplation in the form of a guide, a path to follow, a basic course in self-mastery. It is my desire that in sharing with you in this way, you and I will discover greater truths about ourselves, find the courage to accept these revealed truths lovingly and without judgment, and go forward to complete our lives with the richness and fullness they were intended to be. I will offer you tools and exercises that have worked effectively for me in my life and in my desire to love myself, and therefore others, with greater compassion and less judgment.

Regardless of your age or gender, if you are at that pivotal place in your life where the deeper questions begin to eat at you, this book is for you. You are ready for **Self Love 101**. Myself, I began the questioning in my early thirties. On my own journey I encountered men and women of ages ranging from seventeen to eighty, all asking the same eternal questions:

"What is my purpose in life?"
"Why am I here?"
"What happens to me when I die?"
"How can I find peace?"
"Is there something particular
that I have come to do?"

I believe that there is—something that you came to do. I am also one of those who believe that we live many lifetimes. The spiritualists would say "past lives", the quantum physicists, "parallel lives". Must you agree with me on this subject in order to benefit from this book? Absolutely not! Do try to keep an open mind though. You might be surprised to discover how such a concept makes "all things clear".

If you *are* someone who has pondered the question of purpose, I present to you a possibility. What if your purpose is simply to know yourself and to love yourself as you come to know the real truths about who you are. Even all the "bad" stuff, the dirty little secrets. What if every situation within which we find ourselves, we find ourselves there mainly for the opportunity it presents—**to know and to love ourselves.** The family that we are born into. The circumstances. The place and time. Events that occur near and far. Our friends and lovers. Our spouses. The children born to us. Our many jobs and careers. The challenges. Every encounter, large and small. The teachers, students, teammates. The conflicts. The unfortunate befallings. The successes. The failures. The delights. The dismal drudgery. The passions. The fears. The talents. The journeys, holidays, delays. The accidents. The miracles.

What if finally it doesn't really matter so much what we do or who we are with or where we go? What if what matters most is the consciousness, one could say the attitude, with which we approach the doing and the being with and the going to? What if every person, place and thing that we encounter in every moment, with every breath, is met with the attitude, the consciousness, that this is yet another opportunity to know and love ourselves? What if **that** is the purpose of your life? Yes, you may be called from within to **do** something specific—to be a teacher, a singer, a parent, a successful businessperson, to create this or that. Yes, you may be drawn by heart and soul towards someone and something and some place specific. It is no accident that you are. Be wise and trust. Follow that inclination. Your inner wisdom is wiser than you know. But these things, persons, places, they are the tools, the opportunities, not the purpose. The purpose, I believe, is to know and love **YOU.**

You can best accomplish that by following your inner wisdom, your passions, your attractions, and exploring yourself within these. In every moment there is opportunity. Ask in that moment,

"Who am I in the presence of this? Of that? Of him? Of her?"

Begin to consciously know yourself. Do not judge who you see yourself to be in that moment. Let it be good enough. However ugly or distasteful your ego finds it to be, let it be OK. *"Yes, I am that!"* Yuk! I know. Often it is not pretty what we see. The ego screams *"No, I am not that! I am a good person,*

11

a loving person. That is ugly, evil. No, I am not that!" Observe. Observe your reaction. The intensity of your ego reaction, the strength of your *"I am not that!"* is an indication of the degree to which you judge that—that which is a part of you, like it or not. In the presence of judgment, there is the absence of love. I repeat:

"In the presence of judgment, there is the absence of love."

If the purpose of your life is as I believe it to be, to know and love yourself completely and unconditionally, then try to be grateful that you have been given yet another opportunity to love what you do not love—about **you**. Believe me I know it is not easy. And of course, you don't have to do it. You are free. You are the master of your life. Do it. Don't do it. Love yourself fully or don't. The sometimes hard to accept truth is that there is no one outside of you making the rules, judging you. Not even God. If what we call God exists, it exists as an unconditionally loving state of BE-ing. One can say that this God state already loves you unconditionally. It is YOU that do not. If in fact you don't. You may have already achieved that supreme state of self-love. If so, you would be what is called "enlightened". Good for you. You need not read further. You may go and have tea with Jesus and the Buddha. If, like me, you are not quite there yet but truly want to be, read on my friend. Take a deep breath, ask Jesus and Buddha to save a place at the table, take courage, and trust that you are loved—and lovable.

*   *   *

Knowing yourself and loving yourself unconditionally inherently requires that you look at your conditioning and your belief systems; that you discover what is true for you and why. I was raised Roman Catholic with all of the attendant conditioning. I was devout as a young man, a believer. I even considered entering the seminary at two different times in my life. The beliefs surrounding this religion were deeply imbedded in my consciousness, my psyche. When I first began to awaken to other possibilities, these beliefs, this conditioning, was perhaps the most difficult to let go of. I had had no previous exposure to other religions, to Eastern religions such as Hinduism, Buddhism, Islam, and certainly not to metaphysics and spiritualism. I was an innocent. I believed that what I had been taught was the truth, the whole truth, and nothing but the truth.

And, of course it was. True. What I came to realize early on in my own awakening experience is that there are many perceptions of truth. What is true for you in one moment, one time in your life, becomes limited understanding once you have grown beyond it. As long as it feels true to you, it is, and it serves you in your life. You are attracted to others for whom it is also true (therefore churches, synagogues, temples). They then reinforce the truthfulness of your beliefs. This truth can serve you and satisfy you for an entire lifetime. For the majority of people, in fact, it does. I am referencing religious *truth*, religious belief systems, but this applies to all of your belief systems—moral, political, sexual, and cultural—all of them, including your beliefs about love.

Then one day you are drawn to pick up a book, or a friend sends you a YouTube video to watch, or you have a life-threatening accident, or lose a loved one, and suddenly your truth is assaulted, your beliefs are called into question. Your mind is opened to another possibility. Perhaps just a sliver of light, of awareness, slips past the established belief. You are ready for change, ripe for transformation. A seed is planted. You begin to question, to seek answers to heretofore unasked questions. To wonder. To imagine. You suddenly feel energized, excited, curious again. The status quo no longer satisfies. Soon you find yourself encountering others who are feeling similar feelings, having similar thoughts. More books, videos, experiences come your way. You are thirsty, hungry for knowledge, for understanding. The pillars of your established temple of truth begin to crumble in the light of newly revealed understandings.

Were the pillars therefore never substantial? Never true? Ahhh. But it is not the truths, the pillars, that have changed. It is you. They remain as they were, true to those who view them as such. It is your perception that has changed, that has transformed into something new. Those pillars of truth supported you in your life, served you on your path. Bless them for what they have been to you. Be grateful. If the pillars were called Catholicism and you find that now you cannot abide by these truths, let them be. Do not judge that you once believed. Do not judge those that still believe. You were not wrong. They are not wrong. You have simply taken another step up the ladder, *your* ladder, of personal growth, personal awareness. I repeat: YOUR ladder. We have the tendency at this stage of transformation to feel superior, to have been able to see what they cannot see. They have simply not awakened yet to the real truth. Ah yes, the ego at work. I know. Been there, done that! Every soul has its own path. For one being, the path called Catholicism is the perfect path to attaining self-love, to attaining enlightenment. History has proven it to be so. For another, the path called Buddhism. History has proven it to be so. For another, Islam. For another, Naturism. For another, artistic creativity. For another, science. And so on. Infinite possibilities, countless paths.

In this book, I am sharing with you what has worked for me on my path, what I have come to perceive as true. It is my truth, my path. Hopefully this too will evolve, transform into something greater. Already as I write these contemplations, I witness truths that I had held for some time shifting slightly, transforming. Hallelujah!!! Take from it what feels right for you, what feels true for you in this moment of your life. Be with it. Nourish it with the truths of other paths. Make it your own.

Let your mind be open. Consider the possibilities. Use the gift of right discernment. An open mind is the key to personal growth, to personal transformation. With an open mind all things are possible. A closed mind is the greatest impediment to expanding self-knowledge, self-love. Be willing to change— your beliefs, your truths, your conditioning, your habits and customs, your life. Set yourself free. Do not automatically accept anything that I or anyone else tells you as true simply because it is true for us. Take personal responsibility. Consider with an open mind, a keen intellect, and the wisdom alive within you. Make your own choices. It is YOUR path. Walk it with your own unique style. Dance it if you prefer. There is no one else exactly like you in all of the Universe. Celebrate that, my friend, as you consider the possibilities.

My Master referred to this approach to perceived truth as the presence of the "**Perceiver I**". One could also call it the "**Perceiver Eye**." The world exists as we see it to exist, as we perceive it to be. If we change our perception of it, the world changes accordingly. As we see it. And truthfully, what else is there? Quantum physicists have proven that the atom itself is only what it is perceived to be. Its qualities and behavior alter depending upon who is observing it. Truth, at the atomic level, is only as it is perceived to be. **The "Perceiver I"**. The world is, for me, as I perceive it to be—beginning at the atomic level. OK. I can hear your thoughts. *"No, Tim. The world is as it is. Everyone agrees that it is as it is. It is not just as I perceive it."* Really? Have you ever been one of several persons who witnessed an accident? And in discussion found that each of you has your own truth about what had happened? So, what is really true about that little piece of the world?

Humor me. Do an experiment. Pick some aspect of the world as you know it to be. Consciously decide to change your perception of that particular aspect. Example: Old perception: The world is a dangerous place. New perception: The world is a safe and nurturing place. For one full day repeat often to yourself silently and when possible out loud, *"The world is a safe and nurturing place."* When you go to bed that night, contemplate this phrase. When you awaken in the morning nurture the thought. Begin your day, keeping this thought alive in your consciousness. Yes, your ego mind will argue with you depending upon your conditioning on this issue. Let it chatter. Return to the new thought. Observe your experience of that day as you move through your world. Maintain the new perception. Whose world do you live in now? Which world is the true world?

Notice if your experience of the world around you changes, even in the slightest. This is the power of the **Perceiver I.**

"OK Tim. Yes my perception changed but the physical world did not. It is still as it always was." Hmmm. First, let me say that it is your perception of the world that is most important to you. The rest is "hearsay". You can only know the world through your personal experience of the world. The rest is hearsay. The rest is what we as a race of humans have collectively accepted to be true. The world is flat. Remember that? The earth is the center of the Universe. Remember that? The physical world is as it is because we collectively agree that it is so. I know. If this is a new concept to you, it is a tough one to assimilate, to accept. Don't worry about it. Forget about it. If you are reading this with a fairly open mind something of what I have said will seep into your consciousness. A glimmer of expanded truth. A new possibility. Let it be. But do consider the concept of the **"Perceiver I"** or **"Perceiver Eye"**, the importance of how you perceive your world to be. Go back to that and your experiment. Play with it. This alone can change your life.

Take time to contemplate life purpose in the light of what I have shared with you. My conclusion, after these sixty-some years, is that the purpose of my life has been to truly know myself and to love myself unconditionally. This is a conclusion only recently come to. It is the result of countless explorations and experiences. As I look back upon them all I see more clearly the definition of my own path, the road taken as seen in reflection. This path I can only call the path of self love.

As you reflect back and gaze forward what is it that you see? How would you define *your* life purpose? Can you find a thread that weaves its way throughout? That begins to define your path for you? Do my personal conclusions resonate with you? If your own path is unclear, as yet undefined, does this help you to begin to define your own life purpose? Beyond the human goals and ambitions, is it possible that knowing yourself completely and loving yourself unconditionally are the real reasons for being here at this time, in this life? Do you recognize this as true for you? Only you can know.

CHAPTER III

Trusting the Inner Voice

When I began the contemplations that evolved into this book I was in Florence, Italy. From there I traveled to France, to Nimes in the south. I had lived for a time in this area, Les Cevennes, rugged, Roman, romantic. When I first drove down a winding road into a river valley that I knew nothing of my soul began to sing. I felt that I had come home. This was years ago, in 2001. Strange how we can arrive at a place that we have never been to in this lifetime and feel so much a part of it, so right in being there. I know that you have had this feeling. So taken was I that I returned a few months later to settle in a house high in the mountains in a quiet village. I had arranged an exchange with the owner who lived in England and was going through a divorce. The house was in great disrepair. I offered to clean and paint and decorate it so that it could be offered for sale. In turn, I could live there for several months. It was perfect! And a true adventure as my French was weak and no one in my little village spoke English. I managed well. It was a healing time.

I had been through a rough patch in the previous months. And 9/11 had just occurred giving another shock to the system. My soul needed solitude. I needed to feel safe, at peace. Trusting that sensation of knowing this place, of feeling as though I had come home, I created an expanded experience, one that also strengthened my certainly that I wanted to live and work in

France. Many things were created by my willingness to trust that initial and immediate "knowing".

As soon as I arrived back into the region on this recent trip, that feeling was alive again. I walked the streets and drove the outlying hills and, once again, simply knew. Home. I have learned over the years to trust that feeling. Often it makes no logical sense. Still, I trust. There is this innate wisdom within each of us. You have felt it. And when you trusted it enough to act upon it, miracles occurred. Magic. This is life as it was meant to be. Immediately I made a new friend who had a beautiful ancient stone home in the area, in a small village between Nimes and the beautiful town of Uzes. He invited me to come and stay and showed me more of the region introducing me to his friends and encouraging my already growing sense that this is where I needed to be. No sooner had I left his good company after five glorious days and another new friend appeared; this one inviting me to his home in Avignon and introducing me to the city. More magic. It was as if the Universe was saying, *"Welcome Timothy. You are known here. Friends and opportunities await you. Welcome."*

Invitations to return ensued. Possible places to live presented themselves. I was enthusiastic about the future for the first time in many, many months. I could *see* a future. Life after 60. Because I trusted in and followed this 'calling' to return here I was reborn, rejuvenated. Because I was willing to step outside of my safe, comfortable, routine in Texas—the deadly known—new possibilities unfolded before me. I was so pleased. This was, after all, the reason I had embarked on this journey to begin with— seeking inner transformation through outward movement.

So, two things at work here. First, listening to that small quiet voice within. Second, stepping outside of the comfortable, or not so comfortable, routine. Both are critical in terms of personal transformation, in terms of revealing more of yourself to yourself. The first and most common question that arises with regards to that voice is:

"But how do I know whether I am hearing the voice of my inner wisdom or the voice of my ego?"

It's a good question. The answer:

"Practice, practice, practice."

The first step is to become aware. Become aware of what you are feeling, what your body and spirit is telling you. Will you actually *hear* a voice? It is more of a thought actually, a resonance within your being. When you sense it, hear it, test it. Step forward in the direction in which you are being guided. Remain aware. Remain aware of what is happening in your outside world as a result of responding to the voice and what you are feeling inside as you do so. Be aware of the movement, the flow. As you move forward, does a path clear for you, is there an easy flow? Do apparent obstacles fall away effortlessly? Do you feel a rightness in the movement? If so, you are most likely following your inner wisdom and not your ego. The ego is generally self-serving and fear based. Its response, its direction, is based mostly upon your conditioning and your belief systems. The ego is not wrong, nor is it bad. It simply is. It is an integral part of who you are as a human being and serves you in many ways in your everyday life. This is about discernment. Not about right or wrong, good or bad. Learning to discern which voice you are hearing and then making a conscious choice of which one to follow depending upon your goals. The only way to gain confidence in your ability to discern between the two is through practice. Listen, discern, decide, act, observe.

Listen Discern Decide Act Observe

I might add here that it doesn't hurt to ask for this inner guidance. If you are not in the habit of hearing it, you may need to jump start the process, to awaken the muse within. *"Ask and you shall receive."*

I cannot emphasize enough: **There is no right or wrong in this**. If you follow the voice only to discover that it brings you what you do not want, take note. Do not judge. Review the process. Learn from it. With time and practice you will more readily know which voice is speaking. There is not a "good" voice and a "bad" voice. There is only YOUR voice. The more truly you know yourself, the more obvious to you which voice is speaking. The more that you love yourself unconditionally, the more quiet will be the voice of your ego.

My own story of following that inner voice and returning to southern France gives great example. For some time before taking the trip I had bemoaned the absence of magic in my life, of synchronicity. Once I made the commitment to follow that voice, the magic began to happen again. Let me say it again. Once I made the **commitment,** the magic began. So even as I sat in Texas preparing for the trip, new friends began to appear online, the ideal apartment became available in

Florence, the perfect airline tickets at the perfect price, and so on. I observed the movement, the flow, the ease with which it was all coming together. This confirmed to me that I was on the right track, the right track to accomplish my goal, my goal of further transformation, of reinvigorating my life. I would not have been wrong to have decided not to make the trip. I simply would not likely have achieved my goal.

Believe me I had many logical reasons not to go. In fact, two days before my scheduled departure, my sister, to whom I had been showing property for two years, finally decided to purchase a house. I had a clear choice. I could cancel my trip, represent her in the sale, earn a $3400 commission (which was my approximate budget for the trip) OR I could follow my inner wisdom and let the money go and move forward with my plans. If I had not worked very hard over the past years to "heal" my money issues, I would have been very tempted to stay. I was not. I never even considered it. The ego voice born of "fear of not having enough" was all but silent. The voice of my inner wisdom was clear and resonant. To have chosen to stay would not have been wrong. It simply would have resulted in a different outcome, and most likely not the one I was seeking.

The second step that I was willing to take in order to provoke transformation, to change my life, was to **change my life**. Sounds simple doesn't it? Usually it's not. I had created a very comfortable life for myself in Texas. I lived in a beautiful condo overlooking the bay, with dolphins at play in the early morning. The area itself was tranquil and beautiful. For the time being I did not need to work. I had manifested sufficient abundance to coast for a while, to enjoy my situation, to ponder the future. I live in a small town so daily life was simple. All the conveniences easily and quickly accessible. I had my daily routine, a leisurely one, a few friends nearby, and lots of family. A dream right? Yes, it was the realization of a dream. Initially I reveled in it. In the previous few months I had begun to realize that I had become stagnant, that I was, in a sense, dying in my comfortable "golden cage". I knew that it was time to make a change but I was not called to move anywhere specific or to do anything specific, not a passionate call anyway. There was no big dream unfulfilled calling me into action. And there was another dilemma. I was ready for a change, felt my time here in my little coastal town was complete, AND I was not ready to completely separate myself again from my family, particularly my elderly parents. I felt caught by seemingly opposing desires. And so I sat in my beautiful golden cage. I was not unhappy but I was also not fully alive. I share this with you because it is such a common experience. We experience it with our work, our marriages or relationships, our choice of place, etc. We KNOW we need to change but we also have all the reasons why we cannot. Or we simply lack courage. I was fortunate. I was alone. I did not have a spouse or lover or children to consider. I was essentially only responsible for me. And still I was stuck.

I prayed and meditated, asked for guidance and direction, for signs, for invitations. Nothing. Oh, I explored several things in terms of work and I traveled quite a bit. I returned to Oregon where I had studied with my master and still had many friends. I asked myself, *"Is it here? Is this the place?"* My logical mind said, *"Yes. Of course."* My soul did not seem to be in total agreement. And so I sat. And I prayed. Mind you, when I pray now I do not pray to some unseen God out there or for Jesus to save me from my confusion. I pray to that which is divine within me, that sublime wisdom, peace and love. Certainly I open myself to guidance from Divine Beings throughout the Universe and from angels in my corner. But mostly I look for the answers within my Self. They didn't seem to be coming. I did receive an invitation from my friend, Marie Lise, with whom I had worked in Quebec and Europe. She invited me to join her and her partner at his home on the island of Corsica for 10 days. Nice, I thought, but this is not the answer I am waiting for, another holiday. Two days later while praying once again, that small still voice offered a bit of wisdom. Essentially it said, *"OK Tim, you say that you ask and do not receive. No opportunities present themselves. No invitations. And yet you have been invited. Why are you saying 'no'?* Given that this is the ONLY invitation, why not say 'yes'?"

And so I did. And once I did the ideas and inspirations began to flow. I would expand the trip and make it a journey of discovery. See Florence. Return to southern France. Paris. Morocco. As I have said before, the magic began once I made the decision. Saying "yes" meant of course that I would have to change my life, even if only for 5 or 6 weeks. I would have to be willing to step out of the golden cage and into the unknown. It helped that I was joining friends whom I loved for the first leg of the journey. The remainder I decided to leave somewhat open. I had an idea of where I wanted to go but did not make specific plans. I felt it was important to be somewhat of a gypsy, to be free to follow my intuition, that inner voice. I was excited but also ill at ease. I had been plagued with certain minor health issues these past few years and I was no longer 50. I worried that I would not be up to such a journey, could not hack it. And I was stuck in my comfortable routine.

Routine births complacency. Complacency stifles creativity. The inability to create, to imagine something other than the routine, causes death. Your body may still be alive (for how long?) but your magnificent spirit is slowly dying. You feel it. You know it. And yet you cannot see how to change it. I said a few paragraphs back,

"You want to change your life? Change your life!"

You don't need to divorce your spouse, quit your job, or move to a strange country. Finally, in time, you may choose to do any or all of these but for now, just make a change in the routine of your life. Take a vacation. Visit a foreign country or place. Place yourself in unfamiliar circumstances with people you don't know and who don't know you. Give yourself at least a week. A month is ideal but I understand that many of you cannot do that. Go alone! I repeat: **Go alone**! Unless you and your husband, wife, partner are completely attuned and in the same place asking the same questions, go alone. Break the routine. This includes the familiar everyday relationships. Go someplace that you would not likely go. Place yourself in circumstances that are uncomfortable. Be willing to look into eyes that do not know you. Have an adventure. If there is an inner calling to do something and you have been ignoring it. Do it!

Explore Your Self

This story of mine that I have just shared with you is just one story, one example demonstrating the power of these principles. There are countless stories out there if you need reinforcement. I have many more of my own. It is time now to write *your* own, to live your own. That is the only reinforcement, the only proof that really sticks—your experience of yourself. Begin to listen. Nurture that quiet still voice within, your voice, your wisdom. Test it.

Listen Discern Decide Act Observe

Then, when you are ready, change your life. For a day, a week, a month. Begin. Answer the call. Take a chance. Trust. Your purpose in life is to know and love you. Unconditionally. The signs await you. Opportunities abound. Open your eyes and ears. Look. Listen. Live.

CHAPTER IV

Reclaiming Peace

The Purpose of Meditation

One of the best ways to refine your ability to "hear" your inner voice is to meditate. OK. I hear you. *"Oh no, not meditation! I tried it. I can't do it. It's too hard."* Or too weird perhaps? Too "spiritual"? Too much association with gurus and mysticism? I understand. I've been there. When my own spiritual teacher first began to talk to us about meditation, I freaked. Me, sit with legs painfully crossed, back aching, repeating some mantra in a language I do not even understand? Not this Texas businessman! No way! Not going to happen! Fortunately for me, my teacher was both persistent and patient. With continued practice my body adapted, my mind ceased its chatter, and my spirit soared. It took time and effort but it was worth it.

And where was it that my spirit soared to? Where did I "go" in meditation? Where does one go? Poetically, we can say that one goes home, home to a place that is well known by each of us—a place of peace. A place of simply being. A place of equilibrium, sacredly held between the breath in and the breath out. A place of peace. This place of peace is not a foreign place. It is not some mystical nirvana awaiting our discovery. It is home. It is who we are at the very core of our being, who we have always been. It is the I AM of which Jesus spoke. Not

I am this, I am that. I AM. Still water. Pure BE-Ing. No DO-ing. No THINK-ing. Just BE-ing. At peace. Home.

Because it is a known place, it is not as difficult to get there as you think. Let go of all of the conditioning and programming that you have taken on with regards to meditation. Let it go. Begin anew. Start with an open mind. Really. What have you got to lose but a part of yourself that you are not all that happy with anyway. Start simply if it is new for you. Forget about the perfect posture. Put aside your image of what a meditator looks like. Just be you. Simply sit in a comfortable position, ideally with your spine erect. Lean against the wall or a cushion if you prefer. Be comfortable. Cross your legs or stretch them out in front of you. Sit in a chair if that is better for you. Place your feet flat on the floor or cross them at the ankles. Rest your hands on your lap or upon your legs. Voila! That's it! You are ready to meditate. Of course it is ideal if you can create a quiet environment where you won't be disturbed for 10 or 15 minutes. If the only place you can find such quiet and privacy is the bathroom, then the bathroom it is. Go into the bathroom, lock the door, and sit on the toilet. Why not! Any place where YOU are is a sacred place. If it doesn't smell quite right in the bathroom, light a candle. Best also to ask anyone that you are sharing space with to give you space for fifteen minutes. Not a lot to ask, even from your children.

That is just how simple the approach can be. Are there specific postures that enhance the meditative state? Yes. And there is a scientific reason for them. **Don't worry about it**. You can grow into them if you like. You don't need them. All you need is the intent and the willingness to create the time and space. Once you are seated comfortably on your meditation "throne" simply close your eyes and relax. In the beginning it might help to consciously relax your body. By that I mean to move from your toes to your temples silently commanding each part of your body to relax. Example: *"My toes are relaxed." "My legs are relaxed." "My stomach is relaxed"*. And so forth. Once your body is comfortably relaxed I want you to take several deep breaths into your body. Breathe in through your nose and take the breath all the way down to your stomach. Let the stomach receive the air and be open and relaxed. (Remember: There is no one looking to see your stomach pooching out.) Release the breath. Good. Repeat this deep breathing in and out several times and then allow your breathing to become more subtle, more quiet, easy and natural. Great! To occupy your mind, you might simply think *"Breathing in, 2,3,4"* as you breathe in and *"Breathing out, 2,3,4"* as you are breathing out. This will serve to pull your mind away from the constant flow of thoughts that inundate us. So simple!

The counting serves a bit like a mantra, giving the mind a point of focus, an occupation, a role in the meditation experience. A mantra is simply a word or phrase that serves as a point of focus. No, it doesn't have to be some mystical word or phrase in ancient Sanskrit. Every word and phrase does carry a specific vibration, however, whether you speak it or simply think it. So, certain words and phrases are of a higher vibration, some lower. Those of a higher vibration tend to more easily carry us into the meditative state. Why? Because the meditative state that we are seeking is of a like vibration to the word or "tone" that we are thinking or speaking. Again, it's not complicated. Speak the word, "Hate". Be aware of how you feel when you speak it. Speak the word, "Love". Be aware. Notice a difference? Different vibration. Different feeling. Another good example is the word "God", one of the most powerful words in the English language. We know it. We don't necessarily think of it in terms of vibration or a tone like the sound from a piano but that's what it is. Too much information? Sorry. I understand. I suggest you take a break from reading and practice what I have just given you. I will do the same. Just writing to you about meditation draws me into the desire to meditate. So, put the book down and practice. I haven't taken you deep into the meditative state yet. That's OK. Practice the beginning steps:

Create a quiet and private space (even if it's the bathroom)

Sit comfortably with your spine erect

Close your eyes

Consciously relax your body from toes to temples

Take a half dozen deep breaths into your stomach

Breathing In 2,3,4   Breathing Out 2,3,4

Allow your breathing to become quiet and subtle

Observe your experience

Whatever is your experience, it is perfect. Don't judge it. Observe. When you are ready to read more and to expand your meditation experience, return to me. Meanwhile I will be enjoying my own sweet return to peace!

*   *   *

That was great! You did great! Seriously. I am assuming that you did the exercise of course. If you did not, no judgment! Just acknowledge that you are not ready to go there just yet. Go there when you feel to. And you will . . . . feel to. The seed has been planted. If you are still reading me, the call to return home to the peace that is the essence of who you are will come. Give it time.

Meditation really is that simple. What did you notice once you allowed your breath to become quiet and subtle? Did you taste a few seconds of the possibility of peace? Maybe you slipped deep into a peaceful state? Or perhaps thoughts raced in to fill the void. No matter. Just be aware of your experience. The thoughts, inevitably, will come. Don't judge them. As they come, see them as soft white clouds floating across the sky of your consciousness, your awareness. Each thought a soft white cloud. See them pass. Do not judge them. Love them. They are an essential part of who you are. As you watch them pass, simply shift your focus back upon your breath or upon your mantra. *"Breathing In, 1,2,3,4"*. Simple. The clouds will come again. Observe without judgment. Return your focus to the breath or the mantra. It is a dance. In time, with practice, the thoughts, the clouds, will be fewer and farther between.

To further assist you I have provided a free guided meditation download on my website: www.timothyernster.com. You may find that it is easier for you to enter into a transcendent state when you are guided by my voice. In the long run, you don't want to be dependent but in the beginning the guided meditation can be a powerful tool.

Now you are ready to take the next step. Repeat the process that I have given you, allowing your breath to become more subtle. Keeping your focus on your light breathing we are now going to change the mantra in order to elevate your experience. Now, as you breathe in softly through your nose, you will contemplate the pronoun, "I", as in I AM. You guessed it. On the outbreath, breathing out through your mouth you will contemplate the word, "AM". Remember your eyes are closed, your body is relaxed. You are safe. Your mantra becomes "I AM". Draw each word out through the length of the breath. Good.

Let's add one last element. Remember, your eyes are closed. Keeping the lids closed shift your gaze inwardly up to your forehead. It may help to imagine that you are looking upwards and out of the center of your forehead, just above your nose. As if you have another eye, a third eye, there at the center of the forehead just above the brow. That's it! You are breathing lightly contemplating "I" on the in breath and "AM" on the out breath. Lids closed, your eyes are focused upwards toward the center of your forehead. Wonderful! You may find that your breath wants to become so subtle that it is almost non-existent. Let it go there. Eventually, with practice, the breathing will cease altogether. The breath will become still. Not to worry. You will not die. You will have come home to where you really live. Remember what I said earlier? The place of peace is a place of stillness, of BEing. The place of I AM. Not I am this, I am that. I AM.

Essentially, you have ridden the tone of the I AM mantra to the place of I AM presence. It is that simple. I AM is a powerful mantra. Unknowingly you use it every day—in your spoken word and in your constant thoughts. I am sick. I am tired. I am sad. I am poor. I am happy. I am beautiful. I am rich. I am healthy. Words have power. Thoughts have power. Be aware and use them consciously to create what you want to create in your human experience. The more you begin to sense your alignment to your Divine Self, to the Universe, to God as we call it, the more powerful will become the mantra.

One last comment on mantra. Most of you are familiar with the mantra "OM", even if only as the butt of jokes about meditators. Earlier I spoke about the vibration or tone of words and sounds. "OM" or "AH OM", a more advanced version of the same, carries one of the highest vibrations that we, as humans, can experience. It is not the preferred mantra of serious meditators by accident. It is purposeful and powerful. It is known as the beginning sound. You have heard it referred to poetically and biblically in this way: "First was the word, and the word was made flesh". In the beginning the Creator Force that we call God created the material out of the spiritual through the "utterance" of the word "OM" or "AH OM".

"Gosh Tim, if that is true why aren't you telling us to use AH OM as a mantra instead of I AM?"

Good question. The answer: because I want your introduction into meditation to be both powerful and simple. Notice the similarity in the tonality of both mantras, I AM and AH OM. No accident. The tones, the vibrations, are nearly the same. For some of you, I AM does not carry with it the baggage that OM or AH OM might. Remember: Simple. Simple. Simple. The other advantage for you as a native English speaker is that I AM has appropriate meaning as well as appropriate vibration. I AM indicates stillness, peace. How perfect. How Divine! It is also interesting, and no accident, that the English translation of the words presumably spoken by Jesus in Aramaic is I AM. Example: "I AM that I AM". Stillness. Peace. Oneness. "I AM the Light and the Way". Many believe that the pure translation would be "The I AM is the Light and the Way". Hmmmm.

You are, of course, free to use OM or AH OM if you feel drawn to do so. Trust what feels right for you. In my own meditations I tend to switch back and forth from I AM to AH OM. Both have positive "meanings" to me because of my own personal conditioning. Use what works. More power to you. Literally!

Once again, why do you want to meditate? At the beginning of the chapter I offered it as a tool to be able to better "hear" your inner voice. Meditation does that for you. When you are in the stillness, this place of I AM, your inner voice, your inner wisdom, is more readily available to you. Why? Because that is where your inner wisdom lives. It is from there that your inner voice resonates. This place of stillness, of peace, of the I AM presence, is where you connect with your Oneness with what some of us call God—The Divine Presence within you. Home. That which you are and have always been. **Peace.** The more you return to that place through meditation, the more certain you become that this is true. The more time you spend in that place of peace the more peace you carry back with you into your human experience. It is a point of reference, a place where you can bathe yourself in this vibration. The ultimate goal is to live that state of peace in our everyday human lives. But how can we live it if we don't even remember it, don't know what it tastes like, feels like? We must take frequent dips into this sweet pond of peace, become drenched in its waters, and return dripping wet to our dry and dreary lives until these lives, this expression, resonates with the unqualified certainty:

THIS IS WHO I AM!
PEACE

CHAPTER V

Where is the Freakin' Joy?

Ha. The chapter title makes me laugh as I remember its source for me. We used a different F word at the time but you get the gist of it I'm sure. I was deep into my experience as a disciple of a very demanding spiritual master, living in community with other student/disciples in a Western version of an Eastern Ashram in the mountains of southern Oregon. Up at 4 in the morning to chant and meditate, a breakfast of oats and almond cream, hours of seva (devotional work in service to God and the community), yoga class, a vegetarian lunch, more seva, experiential exercises, hard core physical training, evening meditation, classes in the self-realization process, late night dialogues, a little sleep and it's 4 AM again. It was a demanding schedule and a demanding process as we were asked to look deep into ourselves to discover all the aspects of ourselves that we judged, that we did not love. At every moment. No reprieve. Ever. We were of course also guided by the Master into finding love for those aspects of ourselves. In the presence of his unconditional love the process was more easily facilitated but not at all easy. Most all of us came out of fairly typical American life experiences. These did not prepare us for the new life we had chosen in our desire to find love of self, to find God, to attain enlightenment. It was a fruitful but exhausting process. Our love for the Master was, at times, all that sustained us. It was deep in the midst of this multi-year experience that some one of us uttered the fateful phrase "**Where is the F . . . . ing joy**?" It became a mantra of sorts, invoked with humor, but also tempered with truth.

Finally, during one of the Master's many lectures, he addressed the question. He pointed out that humans are always seeking joy, looking for joy. What will make me happy? What is the key to happiness? We believe that we will be happy when . . . . When we meet the right person. When we have enough money, the new home, more toys. When we become healthy, more beautiful, more handsome, more powerful, more knowing, more enlightened. When we are loved unconditionally. On and on infinitum.

"Joy is a choice that you make, not a thing that you find", he informed us. *"You want joy? You must choose joy! In every moment you are given the opportunity. What do you choose? Sadness? Confusion? Pain? Suffering? Why? When you can choose joy?"*

Oh, you could hear the responses in the minds of the disciples.

"Oh but Master, this happened to me, that happened to me, this was said to me, this was taken from me, he doesn't love me, she doesn't love me."

"Yes", he responded to the unspoken thoughts. *"You have all the reasons. All the justifications. You have every right to feel anything but joy. I know. I understand. And your justifications are killing you. Is it really worth it? To*

be justifiably in pain? To be justifiably dead? For sure, you have every right to be. You are God!"

(In his enlightened perspective we are all Divine Beings, God, living human experiences.)

"But Master", we collectively whined in our human minds. *"These are my emotions, this is what I feel. I have to be true to what I feel, don't I?"*

"You have only to be true to your Self", he parried. *"And your Self is God. And God always gets what he wants. He IS God after all. There is no judgment. You want to feel sad, you get to feel sad. You get to choose. You are free. You are the masters of your lives. But then don't cry out to me, "Where is the f . . . . ing joy?" You are too funny, silly entities."*

Please understand, dear reader, that all of this was spoken with an attitude of unquestioned love, unconditional love. This love emanated from his very being. Please also understand that I am paraphrasing what he spoke many years ago for the purpose of sharing with you my best recollection of this wisdom. I am taking poetic license as we say.

The point he was making has remained with me now for more than 20 years. It is an important part of my personal path to love of self. We are not meant to be ruled by our emotions. We are meant to be masters of them. That does not mean that we deny them. Emotion is energy in motion. It is important that we allow the flow of that energy in our body, in our being. When we judge a certain emotion to not be OK, when we block the flow of this energy, we do ourselves a grave disservice. And, ultimately, we cause danger and damage to our physical bodies. When we crimp a water hose and stop the flow of water the hose will soon become weak at the crimping point. In a similar way, when we block the flow of our emotions, that blocked energy begins to create a weakness in the physical vehicle that supports its movement. At a cellular level. The cells are denied the life giving flow of this energy and they begin to fester. Dis-ease is born. Cancers are born. Illness is born.

All emotions are valid emotions. We tend to judge anger for example. But anger is a powerful fuel for achieving positive results if properly directed. Again, it is energy in motion. Energy is neither good nor bad. It is. In the same way that money is neither good nor bad. It is a question of what you do with it. Anger can be used effectively to create or destroy. It can also be a powerful tool for self-healing as I myself experienced when I was working to heal from pancreatic cancer. All emotions are valid. The key is to allow them while remaining the master of them. Allowing the emotion of sadness does not necessitate dwelling within it. Experience the sadness. Allow the emotion to be true. And then, having felt the emotion, choose. This can be done in an instant. Do we really need to whine and wail and wallow in it for days on end? How does this serve us? This is indulgence NOT mastery. Again, no judgment. But if this is your choice, as the master said, then don't cry out to God, *"Where is the f . . . . king joy?"*

The realization and acceptance that we are the masters of our emotions and of our lives is a huge step forward in the journey to love ourselves unconditionally. Joy is an important and desirable state to live in whilst you make this journey. It will definitely make the journey more in-joy-able. Heh heh. Sorry. Sometimes I get carried away with myself. And I so in-joy it.

The great secret that my master was sharing and that I now share with you is that you do not find joy, **you choose joy**. It is a choice offered to us in every moment. Sure, there are moments when it is a difficult choice to make, when the world is falling apart around us. If, for example, a mass shooter has just taken the life of our beautiful and innocent 6 year old daughter, can we really choose joy? We can. It is not an easy choice but I have seen it taken and only recently. More easily taken are the everyday choices we make as we go about our normal lives. We don't like the weather. Our boss is an idiot. Our restaurant meal is overcooked. The body is weak, tired, ill. These are the opportunities with the biggest payoff. Those daily life choices. This is where you can begin to become more conscious of what you are feeling and to recognize that you can choose to feel differently. This is where you can change your habitual behavior for the better, given that joy is a state you would like to live in.

These small choices will lead, without fail, to a joy-filled life. If then you are struck by one of those devastating loses such as I spoke of above, you will find yourself more able to face them courageously. As much as you may suffer, what lies beneath is a reservoir of joy that can, in time, make you whole again.

You are probably beginning to suspect that the path to love of self is paved with conscious awareness. You simply must rise out of the fog of habitual behavior and unconscious activity into a state of continuous self-awareness in order to even know what you are thinking and feeling and what choices are facing you. You cannot **CHOOSE JOY** if you are not even aware that an opportunity to choose is present. This is a challenge. I know. I know very well. It was one of the greatest challenges I faced personally. But it is essential. In the universe of choices the first and primary choice is to choose to be self-aware. Out of self-awareness all the other choices are made possible.

So, the answer to the question: *"Where's the freakin' joy?"*

It is inside of you waiting for you to consciously choose it. It is inside of you awaiting your calling. It lives there in that sweet place of stillness with its best friend, peace. You are the power that presides over it. At your command, it arises to enliven your journey, to nourish your spirit. With all that you are and in every moment,

Choose Joy!

CHAPTER VI

Law of Attraction—The Whole Truth

Sharing with you provokes many memories. As I write I become lost in them. I also become acutely aware of the breadth and depth of this journey I have undertaken for myself—this journey that I am encouraging you to take for yourself. It has been challenging, enlightening, painful, delightful, glorious and unending. I feel truly blessed by all of it. Sharing with you has also given me renewed purpose in these that we call our senior years. Purpose is essential. With each paragraph I become more and more enthusiastic about not only the life lived but the life to come. Hallelujah!!! Enthusiasm is also essential. I was told once that the word enthusiasm comes from the Greek and means "from the God within". If so, how appropriate. Without question—and here is that vibration thing again—that which we feel as enthusiasm is a life-giving force. The body becomes electric. The cells more alive and animated. This can only be a good thing. So today, happily returned to Texas, I give thanks. And I acknowledge myself for being wise enough to employ the wisdom I have been given over the years. To change my life in order to change my life. To step outside the known. To break from the routine. To say "yes" when the invitations are presented, when prayers are answered. Even if, in the moment, I don't quite see how this answer can be *the* answer. To trust the still voice within. And to have the courage to act. It is interesting,

I think, that having done so I can return to the place of routine, to that "golden cage" I spoke about in the beginning but feel alive and renewed within in. I no longer feel imprisoned for I have changed in the ongoing process of self-discovery.

And I thank you, you who don't even exist as I write these words except as an expected, imagined audience. You are the receptacle into which I pour my wisdom, my experience of journey, my love. I imagine you there, book in hand, excited, frustrated, inspired, annoyed, impatient, innocent. With the power of my imagination and the love that I AM and that I know you can become, I command you into existence. And so you are there. Thank you.

*　　*　　*

OK. The Law of Attraction. I should say the *Laws* of Attraction because, while there is one primary law, there are also sub-laws that support the overriding principle. And it is usually these sub-laws that people are unaware of or choose to ignore in their attempt to manifest or attract to themselves what they think they want. Therefore, NOT getting what they think they want! While the awareness of the Law of Attraction exploded into our collective consciousness (public awareness) only a few years ago with the publication and popularity of *The Secret* and other books on the subject, it is by no means a new law. Far from it.

So, where does the Law come from? Who made it law? We call it a Universal Law but what does that really mean? Well, it comes from God of course! But what if I don't believe in God? Oh! Now that could be a problem. Ha! I am playing with you.

There is simplicity in that answer but what does that even mean, "It comes from God!"? Who is God? What is God? And we're off and running in a direction that we don't need to go. I don't want your ability to benefit from what I am sharing with you to be dependent upon your belief or non-belief in what we call God. Or your definition of what God is. Or mine. Let's see if we can't leave God out of the equation and still answer the questions.

There are certain established and accepted "laws" that exist in our world as we know it to be. They are scientific. That is to say measureable or quantifiable. For us laymen that means that we can prove them. We can count on them. They are applicable. They WORK. When all the variables are satisfied, they WORK. LAW. The law of gravity is the most commonly known to most of us. The laws of planetary movement and placement. The laws of physics and now quantum physics. One of the laws of quantum physics is that like vibrations are attracted to one another. There's that darn "vibration" word again. Sorry. Bear with me, I am not a scientist. As I understand it atoms with like vibrations are naturally attracted to one another. They coagulate. They collect themselves. They come together. Why? God knows! Ha. Playing with you again. From a metaphysical (beyond the physical) perspective we simply acknowledge that "like attracts like". With our newly established wifi consciousness we might say that the two are on the same frequency. OK Tim, but what about the old adage, "opposites attract"? I think it is exactly that, an old adage, a wives tale. Think about it. Where in your life does that actually apply? We think of it mostly in terms of human couples and on the surface it may appear to be true. The reality is that human couples that really work as a couple with longevity and happiness have mutually satisfying goals and ideals. They are on the same frequency. Like attracts like.

As I said I am not a scientist and have a limited understanding of the science of things. But the newly discovered laws of quantum physics now give greater credence to what the metaphysicians have known for centuries. I repeat, newly discovered. These are not new laws. They are the essential laws of creation, of matter and anti-matter or spirit—only recently entering into our awareness. At the core of the new awareness is that everything is more energy than matter. The physicality of the physical is an illusion. Most of what *is,* is vibration, is spirit. That darn word again. Furthermore, vibration or energy tends so seek out like energy or vibration. This is true from the atomic level into the cellular into the coagulation of cells that we then describe as matter. Objects. Bodies. Things. Things that we want to attract, to manifest. Things that aren't things at all but energy. Mostly. Vibration. Mostly. It only makes sense then that if we align our energy, our vibration, to that which we seek to manifest we can use the Law of Attraction to manifest what we want.

Simple right? Yeah. Don't we wish! It is important to be aware that thoughts are power too. Thoughts are also vibration. A thought is a tone even if you don't hear it. You don't hear the transmissions on radio waves (vibrations) do you? Not without a receiver. And, by the way, there are some humans whose "receivers" are so finely attuned that they *can* "hear" thoughts. They are called psychics. Your thoughts are a critical component, a sub-law, of the Law of Attraction. To apply the law you are usually told to do affirmations to empower the attraction. Why? Because words are power too. A word is a tone, like the tone from an instrument. It is vibration. And it is one step up in power from thought because the utterer of the word is Divine even if he/she doesn't yet know it. The enforcer of the law knows it.

So we speak our daily affirmations in order to attract what we want to manifest. We resolutely take our ten minutes to do so. Every day. Resolutely. For thirty days. And dammit! Nothing. The so-called Law of Attraction doesn't work! I knew I could not have what I want! And so on . . . . Do you find it interesting that the fascination with the Law of Attraction has already diminished in the few years since it was introduced to a wider audience? Because it doesn't work? No. Because we were not given the whole truth and nothing but the truth.

One of the truths is that you don't need to learn how to apply the Law of Attraction. The Law of Attraction applies. It's as simple as that. What you need to learn is YOU. You are the grand "attractor". You. Your thoughts, your words, your actions, your belief systems, your conditioning, your habits and patterns, your feelings. Every one of these is and emits vibration. Every one of these is a critical part of the great divine magnet that you are. Example: You cannot "affirm" that a new lover is coming to you, and yet not *feel* lovable, and expect the lover of your affirmations to appear. If you affirm something and yet your deeply established belief around this something is quite the opposite, it will most likely not manifest for you. If you affirm that wealth is coming to you but often throughout your day you speak about what you don't have, what is it that you think will manifest?

Remember when I said in a previous chapter that the path of love of self is first of all a path of self-awareness, of being aware of who you are being in every moment? Who you are being. What you are thinking. What you are feeling. What you are saying. What you are doing. Damn. That's hard. I know. Ever heard of the powerful statement "KNOW THYSELF"? There it is. You are already living the effects of the Law of Attraction. And, forgive me for assuming so, but most of you are living the experience unconsciously. You get what you "ask" for. You just aren't aware of what you are "asking".

The secret that was not shared with you is that all of these components must be aligned in order to manifest a clear and concise outcome, a pure outcome. Otherwise the purity is compromised. What you end up manifesting is a mixed bag, a cartoon character version of the dream, the vision. Often one or more of the components are so powerful, so deeply entrenched in your experience of who you are, that the manifestation looks nothing like the dream at all. And you are left thinking, *"Where the hell did that come from?"* Darling, it came from you. You are the creator, consciously or unconsciously, of your life.

If you want the Law to work in your favor you simply must be willing to look deeply into yourself. You must be willing to uncover your belief systems and closely consider your conditioning. Your conditioning is the influence of your environment, past and present, upon how you think and feel about the world around you. This begins with your parents and siblings. Your teachers become an influence. Your religion. The media. The culture in which you live or have lived. Co-workers. Friends. Society. You are conditioned to think and feel as you do by those and that to which you have been exposed. Conditioning is not a bad thing. It is a fact of life. A sub-law to the great law of attraction. However it does influence what you then attract to you. In order to be more certain to attract what you really want you simply must be aware of the influence of your conditioning and then correct that influence if it does not match up with what you want to attract now.

Belief is simply another form of conditioning, only more strongly adhered to and therefore an even more powerful influence upon what you attract in your life. Again, what you believe to be true is neither right or wrong or good or bad. However if the belief does not align energetically with what it is you are wanting to manifest the manifestation will likely be blocked or deformed when it does arrive. There is a simple but effective exercise that my friend, Marie Lise, often taught in her seminars. It will assist you to become more clear about what your beliefs are. Allot yourself some quiet time. Take several blanks papers and begin to write from top to bottom on the page: "My beliefs regarding X are . . . .". Line after line. Write quickly without a lot of contemplation. Let the words simply flow. Fill up the page, as many pages as you have beliefs that arrive. Another way to make the statement would be, "My belief system around X is . . . ." or "My belief regarding Y is . . . ." Example: "My belief regarding money is that it doesn't grow on trees." One of my favorites as my mother said it all the time when I was growing up. Imagine how that particular conditioning forms an entrenched belief and how believing that would affect one's ability to attract wealth. Once your page or pages are full and you feel complete with the exercise, take time to review what you have spontaneously written. Most likely you will find some of it quite revealing. Once you are aware of the belief you can then consciously decide if that belief still serves you in your life. If not, change it!

And now, feelings. Emotions. Some you might remember the brilliant comedienne Carol Burnet's parody of that overplayed (in its time) song. "Feeelingggs. Nothing left but feeeeelinnnnngss". Oh My. Now I really am showing my age. Seriously though, what you feel is equally important as what you think, what you say, what you believe. Maybe more important. It is another powerful sub-law component of the Law of Attraction. When I first began on my own path to love of self I soon realized that I didn't have a clue what I was feeling most of the time. I lived mostly unconsciously out of my conditioning in repeated patterns of robotic behavior. My primary motivation was the desire to be loved. I was not conscious of that either.

Emotions are energy in motion. E-Motion. As such they resonate from your being heading outward into the world like the great boom of a big bass drum. They are perhaps the purest of the vibrations that you emanate and therefore the most powerful, the most magnetic. Have you ever been told that if you find yourself in the presence of a wild animal always do your best to suppress your fear? Why would that be? Does the wild animal really know that you are afraid? No. They **feel** that you are afraid. They receive the vibration that emanates from you, the vibration of fear. The fear attracts them to you, attracts to you the experience of what you are feeling. It is that simple really. Certainly you know the expression, "You manifest what you fear the most." More evidence of what I am saying. Emotions are pure and powerful vibrational frequencies that attract experiences to you that will satisfy and align to that particular emotion. The good news? Love attracts more love experiences. Compassion felt attracts compassion experienced. Feeling abundant, prosperous, rich brings that experience to you. Please remember though that this is only one of the sub-laws of attraction. You cannot rely only upon your emotional state. You must also be master of your thoughts, words, actions and beliefs.

Last but not least, actions. Do your actions support that which you are seeking to attract, to manifest in your life? I find this most easy to relate to when it comes to manifesting money or greater abundance. If we realign our thoughts, words, emotions and beliefs to support greater abundance but continue, in our daily life, to act impoverished what will be the likely result? You might still manifest greater abundance but how purely will the manifestation match your desires? Best to have all your proverbial ducks in a row. Actions are strongly symbolic. Small gestures can have a big impact. You don't want to go out and foolishly buy a fancy car that you can't now afford as an action to indicate to the universe that you live in abundance consciousness. This will surely backfire. Take baby steps. Treat yourself to small but significant things. Significant to you as representing abundance. Simple acts that reinforce the feeling of prosperity.

During a period in my life when I had little or no money I would often find myself in the beautiful home of a family member or friend, sometimes as a house guest or house sitter. I had no money but suddenly I was living in a proverbial palace. I had created the opportunity to act as if I was already wealthy and prosperous. Wise old soul that I am I did not sit in my palace and bemoan the fact that it was not MY palace, that I could not afford such a place. No. I "put on the coat" of a wealthy homeowner. I lived as if it were true. I gave thanks for being able to live in such beauty and abundance. I loved and appreciated the experience. I acted "as if" and used the experience to fuel a manifestation. What is ownership anyway? While I was there I owned the experience emotionally. Sometimes that alone is the manifestation itself and satisfies the dream. After all most of the "things" that you think you want you want in order to satisfy an emotion. Right?

The phrase "wear the coat of" comes from my Master. He would often remind us that if we want to be something or experience something we should begin to act "as if" we already were this being or already had this experience. In reference to becoming enlightened or a self-realized being he would advise us to "wear the coat of a Christ". Think, speak, and act as if you already are a Christ. (A Christ is simply one who has assumed his divinity and lives it through his human). Ask yourself what that would look like for you and then act as if it is already true—to the best of your ability to do so. Associate yourself with those who have already accomplished what you seek to accomplish, to be. Let their vibrations embrace you, their actions guide and inspire you. Simple but powerful wisdom. Think about how you might apply that in your life in order to fuel the manifestation of your dreams.

A few paragraphs above I mentioned that I gave thanks for the experience that I was having. I expressed gratitude. An attitude of gratitude. This I have found to be a key element in manifesting in life. Be grateful. No matter how miserable you deem your life to be you can always find at least one little thing to be grateful for. Seriously. One thing. If the only thing you can think of is that you are still breathing, so be it. Contemplate that one thing and open your heart in gratitude. Give thanks to God, the Universe, your God Self, whatever the power is to which you are grateful. Think it. Speak it. If this is the only "prayer" you utter all day, let it be the constant prayer. An attitude of gratitude. When I sit for my morning prayer and meditation one of the main parts of this experience is expressing my gratitude for all the blessings in my life and in the lives of those I love. And I don't just think it, I speak it. Words have power remember?

An attitude of gratitude opens the doorway into greater manifestations, into empowering the laws of attraction. Why? It's another one of those vibration things. An attitude of gratitude is an attitude of love, of appreciation. The heart chakra opens. The vibration of love, of gratitude, begins to emanate. As it emanates it attracts like vibration. The body smiles. Joy is experienced in that moment of appreciation. Your body, your being, becomes a resonant magnet for more experiences to be grateful for. It is that simple really. And it begins with an even simpler, "I give thanks for . . . .".

Another tool that I like is a fairly well known one encouraged by many who teach about manifestation. The suggestion is to take a $100 bill and place it in your wallet, purse, or money clip along with the cash you normally keep. It should be visible to you when you go to take some of this cash out for expenditures. Each time you do so, you think about what you could buy with this $100 if you chose to. You choose not to but you could if you wanted to. After a full day you might have seen the bill and had this thought ten times. You could have purchased $1000 worth of things if you had wanted to. These actions reinforce the feeling of abundance and further assure the eventual manifestation. Of course, if you don't yet have even the $100, start smaller. The tool still works.

Two more sub-laws: Clarity and Relaxed Focus of Attention. It is absolutely critical to be clear about what it is you wish to attract into your experience. So often we have only a general idea and that idea shifts and changes moment to moment. We want this and oh yes maybe that. Be clear. Be specific. Remember your thoughts and words are tone. You must set the precise tone, send out a specific vibration, if you want specific results. If you are content with receiving "sort of" what you desire, so be it. In order to become clear take time with yourself. Contemplate. Journal. Write down what it is you want to manifest. Edit it until it becomes absolutely clear to you. Post it on the fridge or in another place where you will encounter it as you go about your day. You want to keep it at the forefront of your awareness.

This I call Relaxed Focus of Attention. The simple truth is that we manifest what we are most focused upon. Remember, the Law of Attraction is always in effect whether you are employing it consciously or not. Right now, as I am writing this, the United States is experiencing a flu epidemic. Every TV news program, local and national, is focused on it, driving it to the forefront of our awareness. According to the Law of Attraction this exaggerated intense focus will have what effect? Right! More people getting the flu. The alarming tone of the reporting tends to create fear. Fear, as I said before, is perhaps the most powerful of manifesting emotions. My response is to turn off the programming. I don't want the flu and so don't want it to be my center of focus. I am not suggesting that you ignore the fact that the flu is out there and spreading. Be aware of it and take whatever steps you feel comfortable with to protect yourself from catching it. Be wise. Do **not** make it the focus of your attention. Bring your relaxed focused attention to what you want to manifest. I assume that the flu in not one of those things.

What do I mean by *relaxed* focus of attention? First, you become clear. Once clear you now have established an intention. Next you begin to focus your attention upon this intention. You think about it. You strategically place little reminders around you. Whatever might assist you to keep the intention always present in your awareness, your thoughts. This does not mean that you dwell upon it. I am not suggesting that you walk around repeating to yourself either in thought or words, *"I am manifesting a new car. I am manifesting a new car. I am manifesting a new car"*. No. You will drive yourself, and others, mad. This is obsession, not relaxed focus of attention. Obsession is powerful but you also have a life to live, work to accomplish, etc. While you are living your life, caring for your children, doing your job, dancing playfully in your mind, in your consciousness, in your awareness, is your vision of yourself happily driving your new car. In your mind you are already there. You are "wearing the coat", acting as if. You might say that what you are wanting to attract, to manifest, lives in the background of your awareness. It is ever-present. It is the ever-present subject of your relaxed focus of attention.

OK. Let's review what we have covered here as regards the Law of Attraction.

The Law is immutable and you are already living it

Like attracts Like

Everything is mostly vibration—wave vs. particle

Quantum physics supports the Law

Self Awareness is key. Who am I that manifests?

Feelings, thoughts, words, actions, conditioning and beliefs are critical components within the Law

Be ever mindful to maintain an Attitude of Gratitude

You must attain clarity and maintain relaxed focus of attention

YOU are the great attractor, master of the Law

Your vibration will attract that of like vibration

Before we leave this subject I would like to offer another perspective. I proposed early in the book that perhaps our purpose in life is to attain complete and unconditional love of self. Certainly that is my personal path. What role then does the Law of Attraction play on this path? Is it important in attaining love of self to be able to consciously apply the Law? Is it important that we are able to consciously manifest what we want in order to know that we are loved and to love ourselves unconditionally? I know that in the early years of my journey it was important to feel self-empowered, to feel that I deserved to be loved. Manifesting what you think you want certainly helps to accomplish that. I think my master used it mainly to give us proof that we truly are the masters of our lives, that, in his vernacular, we are Divine Beings with Creator Power, one with God. It also served as a carrot to motivate us to live consciously, to be aware of ourselves in every moment, to uncover our conditioning and deal with it, to be truthful with ourselves with regards to our belief systems. It was a tool to accomplish greater self-awareness, to truly know ourselves. You must first know yourself truthfully in order to love yourself unconditionally.

For me that is why it is important and necessary to address. As far as getting what we think we want most of that comes from our human ego consciousness. Often once we get it we wonder why we wanted it so badly. It's a conundrum of sorts. If we just accepted ourselves and loved ourselves as we are with whatever we have or don't have we would be already home. All good things would be ours. And yet, as humans we seem to need proof. I know that I did. I have also observed that I am more effective at manifesting some things or experiences than

I am at others. This tells me that while I have achieved a certain level of mastery I am not yet a Master. Like all of you I am a work in progress. My instrument (me) is not yet pure. I have also observed that as my love of self becomes more present I find myself more at peace. I no longer want or need things and experiences to the degree that I once did. I am more at peace with what is. This is what I wish for you. Use your dreams and desires as a carrot to clear away the clutter, to make pure the instrument, to truly know yourself and to love all that you come to know of who you are. From my vantage point, I can say that it is well worth the effort.

CHAPTER VII

Overcoming Victim Consciousness

I am the Master of my life

"I am the Master of my life" is a strong statement. It is also a necessary one to make if indeed your purpose in life is to truly love all that you are. It is the supreme statement of self-responsibility.

> *"OK Tim, but I am clearly NOT the master of my life. That is something that I would like to be but it is not something that I am. Not yet anyway. Not even close."*

I hear you. But remember last chapter's teaching on "wearing the coat"? Ahh, yes. Acting "as if"? Right. And remember the power of words, the power behind the spoken word? Now you're getting it. Go back to the chapter on meditation and remind yourself also of the power of the statement "I AM". Good. You want to become the master of your life? Begin by declaring it as so.

> *"But isn't this a lie? Given that I am not the master of my life?"*

No. It is the truth. You ARE the master of your life. You are just not behaving as if you are. (Assuming that you are not). Declaring it creates a space for the truth to be "realized".

Applying the Law of Attraction, we can say that declaring it will attract to you the experience of it being a lived experience in your human life. Think of all we have discussed in the previous chapter. The big secret of secrets is that you *are* the master of your life. By your thoughts, emotions, words, and actions you attract to you your life experiences. One can say then that you are responsible for your life as you experience it to be.

This is probably the most difficult to accept of all the truths, of all the teachings, that I will share with you. The reaction of most people is tangible, forceful. As I imagine you reading this I can literally feel your mind and body react. I can feel your body tighten with indignation and certainty as the emotions rise within you and the mind bellows a bold and belligerent "NO". I understand. You have every justification to respond in this way. Most all of your conditioning has taught you otherwise. From the time you were a small child you have been declared to be a victim, almost never a master. Unless, as an adult you have already been walking your path toward self-knowledge and self-love, you have rarely been exposed to the idea that you are responsible for how you experience your life.

The consciousness of victimization is the overriding tone of collective consciousness. It is the consensus of public opinion, public belief. The idea of being a victim is the accepted idea. Amazingly this idea is pretty much universal. It is not an exclusively racial, religious or national concept. It is widely accepted in pretty much all societies to be *"the truth"*. Pretty ballsy of me then to state so unequivocally that it is not. Ha! I will expand my ballsiness by further stating that the majority of humans living in the world, whatever their race, religion, or national origin, do not truly know and love themselves to the extent that I am encouraging you to do—unconditionally. This is an observation, not a judgment.

The consciousness of victimization is also the primary reason we remain stuck in the muck and mire of human misery. Of all of the issues we face as we attempt to love ourselves unconditionally it is the most difficult to overcome, the most intransigent. Why is that? First, most of us believe in it so powerfully. We deeply and strongly believe that we are the victims of people, things, and occurrences. From the smallest to the most profound. Personal slights to natural disasters. Crimes of neglect to acts of terrorism. We know it. The media constantly confirms it just as we do to one another. We are very supportive of one another in our consciousness of victimization. Even our priests, preachers, rabbis and mullahs promote the belief.

The second reason it is so difficult to overcome is that most of us don't want to overcome it. We like feeling the victim. It gives us justification for the existence of all that we do not like about our lives, all that we do not love. We have someone, something, to blame for our misery, our unhappiness, our lack of fulfillment, the absence of joy. We are absolved of responsibility. It is because of **them**! If it is because of them then we can also further deflect our misery by attacking them in retaliation. And we are justified. Rather than take responsibility for our pain, we can focus our anger and resentment on them. We can distract ourselves from the true source, the one who can heal the pain and restore the love. Ourselves.

In our world we are almost never encouraged to stop and ask ourselves how it is that we might have attracted this person or this situation to ourselves. How, consciously or unconsciously, we might have created it, attracted it into our experience? Almost never! Instead, we are encouraged to hire an attorney. "If you have been the victim of . . . .". How often we see this advertisement on TV. This is a reflection of the collective consciousness. You, in your desire to love yourself truly and unconditionally are fighting an uphill battle. Chances are that if you are still reading this you are up for the fight. The collective consciousness can be changed. It is up to you and me. But, if you feel that you don't want to believe that you are not the victim, this is why. You are not encouraged to. Quite the contrary. You are encouraged to declare yourself as victim.

I'll make a suggestion. The next time you find yourself in a situation where you feel that you are the victim of someone else's action, take pause. Become aware of just how this feeling feels in your body, this feeling of being the victim. Where is the emotion? What is the emotion? I am not talking only about the feeling of anger or resentment. Those are the surface emotions. Go deeper. What are you feeling beneath those emotions? If you can get there, most likely what you are feeling is "unloved".

Are you feeling peace? Love? I doubt it. The peace and love is still there but you have allowed your reactive behavior—the anger and resentment—to pull you away from it. You have given away your peace in favor of a feeling that is comfortable in its familiarity but will not fuel your journey to love of self. Many of us are addicted to those "negative" feelings. We are so addicted that we literally seek out ways to stir them up. We seek out confrontation and the opportunities to feel justifiable victimized. Given what you now know about the

Law of Attraction imagine what unfolds. More and more of the same. The feeling of anger, the feeling of victim, is a powerful feeling. You feel it tangibly in your body. As it surges up in your body, the magnet becomes supercharged. You find yourself in an endless whirlwind of catastrophes. You become the ultimate victim of a miserable life.

This is not the path to peace. This is not the path to unconditional love of self. And this is why I stand by my statement:

"You cannot know peace and unconditional love of self if you believe that you are the victim of anything".

You cannot be both the victim and the master. You must choose. I do not say that it is easy. The conditioning is strong and deep. The collective consciousness does not support your dream. Often, your family and friends don't either. That is why you must take courage and declare it:

"I am the master of my life."

In so doing you begin to attract to you the people and the experiences that do reinforce and support your dream.

Another secret. Taking responsibility actually feels good. Another test. This time when you have an incident wherein you naturally react in your victim mode, again take pause. Just as an experiment, choose in that moment to take the attitude, *"I am responsible for what is occurring. I am not the victim. I am responsible".* You do not need to see how you are responsible.

Just pretend that you are. Accept that, somehow, you are. Take a few deep breaths and allow the anger and resentment that wants to arise begin to dissipate as you contemplate that you are responsible, that you have created this, attracted this experience. How does *that* feel in your body? Chances are that it begins to feel good. You begin to feel more powerful and somehow more at peace. Interesting. How can that be? It can be because it is true. And deep down in the core of your being you know it is true. You are the master of your life.

If you can then allow yourself to begin to consider how it might be true, how you might have attracted it, consciously or unconsciously, you are on your way. Initially, the answers may or may not come, but you have opened the doorway. With each new experience, with each new choice of master over victim, you will gain greater appreciation for how good it feels to assume responsibility. And you will begin to see how it is true, how you are responsible. You will feel more empowered and you will feel greater love of self. Once you accept responsibility for having created your life to be as you experience it to be you then own the power to change it. That is the big pay-off.

There is an advanced tool or process that I call **Intent & Outcome** that can very effective in assisting you to look deeper within yourself and discern the true intention behind your manifestations. First, you must be willing to "assume" that what has occurred or appeared in your life has been birthed from within YOU—that you have created it, consciously or unconsciously. You assume, you accept, that this is the way in which life manifests. You then look at what has appeared, the outcome. If the outcome is, for example, that you have lost your job, you begin with that. That is the manifestation. That is what you have created, attracted. Most likely, unconsciously.

"But, Tim, it was not my intention to lose my job. I need my job!"

I hear you. Begin then to contemplate your thoughts and feelings regarding your job, your work. How were you feeling about this job? Did it truly serve and satisfy you

"Hmm. No. Not really. I have been dreaming of doing something entirely different, something that is more me."

Interesting. And?

"Well, there were financial risks involved. Even if I didn't love my job at least I know I had a paycheck coming in. Even though I was unhappy, I couldn't commit to making a change and losing the security. I was afraid."

Now we are getting there. Your dream, your intent, was to change your life, to move into work that is more satisfying, more fulfilling. Your dream also includes doing that with minimum risk, doing it in a way that works smoothly in transition. That is your pure intent. So what happened? How did the manifestation of the dream become distorted? How did the outcome come to look like getting unexpectedly fired? To answer that question we have to look at the other influences that effect the manifestation. I am not talking now about influence from the outside—the boss, the economy, etc. I am talking about influences from within you, you the master of your life.

First, the fear. I have said before that fear is a powerful manifesting emotion, perhaps the most powerful. When fear becomes mixed up with the dream the outcome can become distorted. Remember, fear attracts that which you fear. Like attracts like. The dream of changing into new and more fulfilling work at your own timetable is influenced by the fear of not having enough money, etc. The outcome will reflect which is the stronger, the fear or the dream. In this example, the fear of lack created exactly that. No job, no income, before creating the dreamed of new career. However, you now also have created the opportunity to make that change, ready or not. The dream was not lost in the shuffle. The fear simply altered the precise outcome. There would normally be other influences of course and you would want to look at all of these, going deeper and deeper into yourself—your emotions, thoughts, and actions regarding the pure intent and all that it entails.

It is critical to be aware of all. If you are aware of the fear, and you were in this example, you can manage that fear. You can work with it, appease it. Use the power of your mind to wrestle with it. Work through the scenarios, feel the emotions, breathe through them into a place of trust. Remember, beneath the fear of lack of money lies the fear of death. I will give you a tool with which to face that fear in a later chapter.

Again the purpose of **Intent & Outcome** is to assist you to see how you manifest what you manifest. How the pure intent becomes altered in the process. How, if you are willing to look deeply, you will see all of the influences and can, in future, more clearly match the outcome with the original pure intent. You can then more readily accept that you are NOT the victim. You are the master of your life.

*   *   *

"OK Tim, I can begin to accept how in these personal experiences and apparent victimizations I am possibly responsible. But what about the larger, grander, issues? Am I not the victim when it comes to war, terrorism, natural disaster, disease, illness, the failure of the economy, etc.? Suppose I was born into poverty or slavery or into an abusive family situation. Am I not the victim of these circumstances?"

There are two answers to these all-important questions. First, you are a part of what I have been calling the collective consciousness. Your individual consciousness is your awareness. It is more than just your thoughts. It incorporates your beliefs and your emotions. It is how you view the world around you and yourself within it. The collective is simply the grouping of individual consciousness. The family in which you live has a collective consciousness. The community in which you live has a collective consciousness. The same is true of your country and, finally, the planet. What you think, believe and feel feeds the collective. To the degree that you are a part of that collective, you are also responsible for it. In the language of the spiritual, *"We Are One"*. Again, quantum physics confirms it. In quantum reality we are not separate bodies or beings. We are all connected by webs of atomic stringlets. We do not see them, most of us, but they are there. We are, in essence, one atomic body, a body that is more spirit than matter. Our thoughts, beliefs, emotions, our consciousness, are also atomic in nature. These atomic vibrations are interconnected within the collective and create the collective consciousness of which I speak.

When we speak poetically that "No man is an island", we speak a great truth. We are all part of a collective. Did not Jesus teach, *"I am my brothers' keeper"*? *"What is done to the least of my brothers is done unto me"*? Spiritual truths and mystical teachings are supported by science. WE ARE ONE. The collective consciousness expresses that oneness. The collective consciousness is also subject to the great Law of Attraction. Thought manifests. Belief manifests. Emotions manifest. Actions manifest. The manifestations occur on a scale appropriate to the size and range of the collective—familial, community, national, worldwide. Given that we are a living part of that collective we are responsible, in part, to what is manifest from it, what is attracted to it.

Darn it. You just can't escape it, can you? You don't want to be responsible, nor do I. It's too much to accept. It can't be true. Let me at least be the victim of war and hurricanes. Give me that at least. OK. I'll make you a deal. I might give you a pass on being responsible for what happens on a global level if you will at least accept that how you respond or react to what happens **is** your responsibility. How about that? Remember the teaching about "Choosing Joy"? In every moment we have the opportunity to choose how we respond to the world around us? Being a master of your life is also about mastering how you experience your life. After all, your personal experience is really your only reference, right? The rest, remember, is hearsay. If you cannot take partial responsibility for what happens in the world, you *can* take responsibility for how you react to what happens. You can choose to react with love, with joy, with compassion, with forgiveness rather than with fear, vengeance, anger, hatred, resentment. Those choices influence the whole, the collective, and the manifestations to come. How about that? Then let the rest of it simmer in your consciousness. Let simmer the idea that we are truly one being, one consciousness, and that as such we each play a role, a responsible role, in what is happening and what is to happen in our world. I'll settle for that.

The second answer responds to the question about circumstances of birth. It also applies to the issues of global manifestations as well. I cannot answer that question without addressing the concepts of karma and reincarnation. I wish I could because I know that some of you don't want to hear it but I simply don't have another answer. I have looked for one. I have looked and pondered and studied and wrestled with it for decades. I find no other way to even begin to explain life as we know it to be if I choose to ignore the effect of karma or the concept of reincarnation. The only thing that makes good sense to me is that we have lived many lifetimes in our journey back to pure love of self. The judgments of actions taken in those lifetimes, if not resolved within that lifetime, are carried in the soul into the next lifetime. Note that I said the **judgments of actions**. It is not the actions themselves that result in karma. Karma is generally defined as *"You reap what you sow"*. I propose to refine that definition to state, *"You reap what you sow and have judged that you've sown"*. If you take an action, even one that we would consider heinous or evil, and do not judge it, there is no karma. There are no amends to be made. There is no karma to balance. Peace is maintained within you. It is the judgment of those actions that is stored in the soul from which future situations are created in order to give you the opportunity to make peace with what you have done in the past.

The past is not limited to a given lifetime. The soul houses the "spark of life" that you are. The soul is also your vehicle to move from one lifetime into the next. It is also the vehicle that houses this spark of life and the consciousness that you are, in between lifetimes, in a space of existence that we generally call "heaven". It is another dimension of reality, a spiritual world where you have the opportunity to review your previous life and lives. From this heavenly estate you are able to view the bigger picture as it were. You are also more in touch with the Oneness, Peace and Love that you are. (Some would call this God). In your continuing desire to live this Oneness, Peace and Love in the human experience you take note of the actions from previous lifetimes judged and held in your soul. Your desire to make peace, to create harmony from the imbalance, propels you to take another lifetime in order to encounter the souls that you have "wronged" in your own judgment or to live differently an experience. That, for me, is the experience of karma. Even if you don't wholeheartedly agree with it, you have to admit that it does help to explain why imbalances, injustices, are often not seen to be resolved in the course of one lifetime, why some seem to "get away with murder" for example.

What about general life situations that you are born into? Some possibilities to consider: You might have judged how you treated the poor and therefore choose to reincarnate into poverty in order to gain compassion. You might also have judged "all those rich people" and choose to create a life experience in which you become one of them. You might have been the enslaver, the murderer, the rapist and, having judged those experiences, seek to return and reclaim your peace. This is a simplification of course but I hope you begin to have an understanding.

I will end my discussion of karma and reincarnation here for now and pick it up again in a future chapter. I have shared enough of my thoughts to either cause you intense reaction or considered contemplation. It is possible, of course, that I am totally wrong about all of this. However it is essentially what the masters have been teaching for millenniums. Do try to keep an open mind. Ultimately you must arrive at your own truth about these and all things that I share with you. After all,

You are the Master of Your Life

CHAPTER VIII

Sexuality

Whew! Sometimes the contemplations on how life really is stirs the soul into a state of anxiety. Looking out and back upon the experience of mastery vs. victimization is difficult, even for me. So many memories. So many challenges faced along the way. Pain is reawakened, revisited. Choices that I have made reconsidered. For the most part I am pleased. The preference of mastery over victimization has been liberating, empowering. I sit at my laptop remembering, reflecting. I seek to share some of what I have found to be useful, necessary, and integral to my own realization of love of self; to the degree that it has been realized. I am both disturbed and illuminated by the remembering and the sharing.

I once asked my Master what was my dharma, my life purpose, in this lifetime. As always his response was *"You have come to know that you are loved, to know that you are God".* *"Yes"*, I pressed, not satisfied, *"but what have I come to **do**?"* He smiled upon me indulgently, understanding my very human need to believe that there was something specific that I came to do. Not enough for me to come to know that I am loved? *"Feed humanity"* was the simple and enigmatic answer he gave. I thanked him but left his presence thinking, *"Feed humanity? What the hell does that mean? Start a soup kitchen?"* Ha. I was not at all pleased with the answer.

Many long years later, long years of attempting to accomplish his first answer, love of self, I hope that I am also accomplishing the answer to his second, feed humanity. For that has become the reason for these pages, this sharing of wisdom that I have gained in my own desire to love myself wholly and unconditionally. The fruits of my long journey. Food for humanity. I know that for some of you the food is hard to digest. I understand. Be gentle with yourselves. Take what you can of it. Digest it slowly. What is repugnant to you, you may leave on the plate. Believe me, there was much that I was fed by my teachers that I absolutely and determinedly refused to partake of. I reacted and rebelled. Often I cast the plate aside arrogantly. The teacher and the food were unaltered by my very human reactions. In time the plate was passed my way again. Finally, humbly, I would partake and give thanks. This is a journey of self-discovery. It is not my desire to convince you of anything. If it doesn't agree with you, don't consume it. You are free. It is, finally, *your* journey of self-discovery, *your* path that you walk. I feed you the fruits of my own experience in the desire that it will aid you on your path. It is my *dharma*, and my great honor and pleasure to do so.

Speaking of pleasure, let's now talk about sex! That should lighten the mood a little. Sex and the path to self love? Really? Really. Remember I have said that one must know oneself truthfully and love oneself completely. That is without exception. Our sexuality is an integral part of who we are. Because of the conditioning of society and religions it is also a part of ourselves that we are most likely to judge. Remember:

**In the presence of judgment there
is the absence of love.**

On my own path the judgment of my sexuality was perhaps the most severe of all of the judgments that I held upon who I was. And there were many. But sexuality? In my case the judgment was mainly about sexual orientation, but not exclusively so. Sex in general was not altogether OK. That old conditioning again. In this case both parental and religious. I grew up Catholic in the 50's. Need I say more?

I will of course. Say more. Let me continue by first saying this:

We are spiritual beings living a physical experience.

That's right. Spiritual beings—that spark of light housed within the soul—the consciousness that I have spoken of. The soul. These are things of spirit, not matter. We, this spirit, this consciousness, take physical bodies to experience the physical plane, life on planet earth. We do so for many reasons not the least of which is to experience the pleasures of the human body. To feel the wind, smell the flowers, taste the wine. The touch of a soft hand or a strong one. A kiss so sublime. Sexual intimacy. These we cannot experience as spirit, as consciousness. We must become physical, become human. And so we do. By choice I might add. None are here by accident. It doesn't happen. Sorry. You don't get to play the role of victim here either. You have chosen. Having chosen why would you then judge the experiences that you came to experience? Including the pleasures of the body.

Don't do it. Let it go. Meet your conditioning head on. Address your belief systems. Trace it to the source. Understand why you feel the way you do and then choose. Choose from a place of self-love what you want to feel about it now. Reclaim peace. I do not mean to suggest that this is an easy choice, an easy journey. For me it was a long and living hell. It is so for many, regardless of their sexual orientation. I chose to take the hard road. I chose to be born gay in mid-century America to conservative Catholic parents in a small south Texas town. What was I thinking up there in heaven? Ha. I think it must look so much easier from that elevated vantage point. *"Hmmm. I'll just add homosexuality to the bag of characteristics I'll embody this time around. See what that contributes to the journey toward pure love of self."* Right.

From this vantage point, reflecting upon my life at the age of 64, I would say, *"Smart move Tim"*, but I certainly did not feel that way for much of this lifetime. I can say it now because I can see the beauty of it, the wisdom in it. To be oppressed from such a young age by such self-judgment? To feel for so many years that I was sick, dirty, sinful? Unloved by God who surely knew the truth about me. Remember, this was long before gay liberation was even thought of. The word gay was not even a part of the language where I grew up. You were a queer, a pervert. You were disgusting. Not that I was doing anything gay. I was not, did not until I was in my late 20's. But I knew. I knew and I hated myself because of it.

I now believe that we choose such "burdens" in order to compel us with a force monumental to overcome, to prove beyond all of society's evidence to the contrary that we are worthy to be loved. It's like compressing a spring to its complete tightness and then releasing it to spring forth into its full potential. It is also likely that in a previous life I had held strong prejudice against homosexuals, possibly persecuting them. The choice would allow me the opportunity to make peace with that, to balance the karma. That is speculation of course because I do not remember.

I offer myself and my homosexuality as an example to illustrate. I began to allow myself homosexual experiences in my late 20's but still with considerable judgment. Liberation had come but not for all of us. So too had AIDS. God's wrath it was said to be. As if we didn't all have enough self-judgment already. Soon I encountered my first spiritual teacher whose teachings cast salt upon the wound. Essentially he taught that homosexuality was a mal-alignment against nature; that it was not the way human expression was meant to be. He insisted further that because we knew this was true in the depth of our being, we could not participate in these acts without judgment. The self-judgment, he said, was killing us. The killing had arrived forcefully and we called it AIDS.

So much for enlightened wisdom. I bought into it because it confirmed what I already believed and headed straight into the arms of a woman. That did not work out well of course. Soon after, I encountered another teacher who became and is today my true spiritual master. His teachings were more enlightened and he aided me unfailingly in making peace with my homosexuality. I believe that the pain of my self-judgment drove me with a passion to find love, to find understanding, to find peace. First to one teacher and then another. It was the driving force but the other areas of self-judgment were then also addressed. It also drove me into the presence of a master who embodied unconditional love. In that way this intense self-judgment of sexuality was my savior.

This can be true of any aspect of ourselves that we judge. These can be the tools, the fuel with which to propel ourselves toward love of self. First, we must accept them. Acknowledge that, yes, this too is who I am. *"Know thyself."* With great compassion towards self we must then find a way to love these heretofore judged qualities, to find forgiveness. Forgiveness is not *"I am sorry. I am sorry. I am truly sorry."* Forgiveness is acceptance of what is without judgment. Forgiveness is loving what seems to be impossible to love. Remember when I proposed that perhaps what we call God is simply a state of BEing unconditional love? This state of love unconditional is the ultimate goal of this particular path. The accomplishment of that state begins with allowing love for that which you have heretofore judged as un-lovable. About yourself. No conditions. No qualifications. Only when you have accomplished pure unconditional love of self can you love unconditionally the world around you.

Sexuality is, obviously, only one piece of the puzzle that you are but it is a critical one. First, we all have it. We all share this piece of the puzzle. We are all, among other things, sexual beings. Second, most all of us have some level of judgment on this piece of the puzzle. Again, with good reason. It is called conditioning. Unless we acknowledge this judgment and choose forgiveness, we cannot love ourselves wholly and completely. We cannot accomplish what I propose to be the true purpose of our lives. Only you can know where you stand on this issue, what you feel about your sexuality. I encourage you to take the time to look deeply and the courage to be truthful with yourself.

Again, we chose to be born into the physical in order to enjoy the physical. We are also now choosing to also be the masters of our lives, to not be the victim of anyone or anything. This should include your enjoyment of the physical. Addiction is not enjoyment. You cannot be both master and addict. Most of us also cannot be addicted without judgment. If we are addicted to food, tobacco, alcohol, drugs we are not in mastery. If we are addicted to certain emotions we are not in mastery. If we are addicted to violence we are not in mastery. If we are addicted to our sexuality, our sexual appetites, we are not in mastery. And, chances are, we are not in non-judgment of self. It's possible. Not likely.

Our sexuality can also serve as a great gateway. The incredible intimacy of the sacred act of sexual congress is unique within our human experience. When else do we physically enter into the body of another human or receive into the body the body of another? When else do we enjoin ourselves so completely? When else do we experience such oneness with another through the physical? Only in sexual congress, in making love. It's a revelatory phrase, *"making love"*. In our experience of sexual congress we are *making* love, expanding love. The union is more than physical. Our energies, our vibrations (there's that darn word again) are enjoined, comingled. When the enjoining of these energies is conscious the power is magnified profoundly. That is to say that when both parties are consciously aware that they are enjoining their energies, their vibrations, their spirits, as it were, the act of making love becomes an experience of transcendence. It transcends the physical realm. It becomes a spiritual experience. You experience a state of transcendence, of slipping beyond the physical world. You transcend the physical into that same space of love and peace that you are carried to in meditation. Poetically, we would say that you go to God, the God within you. In a moment of ecstasy you become lost to your physical self and experience yourself as the unconditional love that you seek to become in the physical. What a great tool! Making love. Conscious sexuality. And what fun!

If you know about or take the time to learn about what we call chakras or energy centers in the body, you can further fuel this amazing experience of yourself. The most common understanding is that there are seven energy centers or energy vortexes aligned to our physical bodies:

Root Chakra—at the base of the spine

Naval Chakra—at the naval area

Solar Plexus—at the solar plexus (duh)

Heart Chakra—at the region of the human heart

Throat Chakra—you guessed it

Third Eye Chakra—between the eyebrows and raised
   a bit

Crown Chakra—at the top of the head

They are often given specific colors and might be seen as flat rotating discs of energy like a large CD disc dissecting the physical body at these locations. There is much wisdom out there regarding the chakras so I will not go into detail here. This is sufficient information for you to utilize them in enlightening your sexual experiences.

It is a simple process. As you are preparing to make love, you and your partner first sit back to back and consciously open your bodies' chakras and align each to each of the other's in sequence, base chakra up to crown chakra. To open simply means to contemplate them, to envision them as alive with energy. Aligning them means to imagine these swirling disks of energy to comingle, to enjoin themselves just as you are about to do in the physical. Very simple. Very powerful. The sweet journey to ecstasy is jump-started and intensified. A side note: Ever notice your tendency to exclaim *"Oh God!"* when in the ecstasy of orgasm? Maybe you already know at a deeper level something that you didn't know you knew—that within the very human enjoyment of the sexual, of making love, awaits also the deeply longed for return to the experience of Oneness, of yourself as love unconditional, of what some of us choose to call God.

I encourage you to allow your sexuality to be yet another of the tools that you have at your disposal to rediscover love of self, to reclaim peace. Look honestly at your thoughts, feelings, beliefs and actions regarding your sexuality. Discern for yourself which of those you judge, which of those you do not love. Either come to love them or let them go. Become the all-loving master of your life that I know you to be.

CHAPTER IX

Man in the Mirror

Long years ago, when I was living and studying in my master's ashram, Michael Jackson released his hit single, *Man in the Mirror*. Immediately we adopted it as one of our many "anthems" to rally us along on our path to love of self. Yes. Michael Jackson. In our sacred temple, the huge speakers resounding with his voice and music, we would dance like disco divas. I know. You would think that in an ashram we would be listening to Buddhist monks chanting. We did. But we also moved our bodies and spirits to the music of those popular artists whose words inspired us. And, believe it or not, moving the body in joy and celebration is also a great prelude to meditation. You get the energies swirling to the point of exhaustion and then "bam", stop the dancing and sit. As your rapid breathing begins to settle you are more magnetically drawn into the meditative state. Chaotic meditation. It works. Try it. You'll love it!

Now, Michael Jackson, like most of us, had many personal flaws. He was, however, at one level deeply attuned to his inner voice, the abiding wisdom and love within him. This was a part of his genius. This particular song was perfect evidence of that.

"I'm starting with the man in the mirror.
I'm asking him to change his ways.
If you want to make the world a better place,
Take a look at yourself and make that change."

This states so eloquently the teachings I received from my teachers and what was then confirmed in the living I have done since. Here again we are brought back to the concept of self-responsibility. Metaphysicians like to say, "Nothing really exists outside of ourselves". This is tough to swallow, difficult to conceive, because it darn sure looks like nearly everything exists outside of me. The whole world is "out there". I agree. It's best to not go there.

I prefer to view it differently. I believe that:

The world around me reflects to me what I most need to see about myself in order to know myself completely and love myself unconditionally.

The world around me is my mirror. This touches on what I have written before when I reminded you that you are the master of your life. Even Michael Jackson knew the truth: If you want to change the world around you, first change yourself. This is also why I said in the beginning of these reflections that you don't need a guru, a teacher, a master. The immediate world around you *is* your teacher—if you allow it to be. The immediate world around you will mirror to you that which you love and do not love about YOU. The best way to change that world, should you want to do so, is to change yourself.

At one of the many weekend seminars that my teacher gave before establishing his ashram we spent the entire three days wearing a hand mirror tied to a ribbon around our necks. Can you guess the purpose? Of course. Man in the mirror. A constant reminder that the world around us is a reflection, that it is not finally about him or her or them. It is about me. We even had to sleep with them tied around our necks. During the day we received many related teachings but in order for the teachings to penetrate we wore the mirrors. It was very effective. There were over a hundred in attendance. During the course of the three days there were many types of encounters, some occurring naturally, some orchestrated by our teacher. Emotions during such events run high. There are plenty of opportunities to react to others—their words, their actions, their manner. The typical human reactions. Always about **them.** But then there was that damn mirror. Just hanging there. And right over the heart chakra. A constant and annoying reminder. It's not about them, Tim. Look in the mirror. Just who is this man in the mirror being reflected back to you? Who indeed!

Very soon we realized that we had not just one teacher but over a hundred. Everywhere we looked. No place to hide. The world around us. Inescapable. Of course, we could refuse to look. We could refuse to play the game. But we were there because we wanted something more than what we had so far experienced in our lives. We called it by different names—enlightenment, God, love of self, peace. We wanted change. And though we were afraid, we still wanted to know ourselves truthfully. We wanted to look in the mirror, hoping to find beauty and goodness and light. That was, of course, not always what we found. The person in our face was angry or judgmental, self-important or sarcastic. He or she was at war—with everything and everyone. She was abusive. He was manipulating. On my part the rush to judgment was quick. And then there was the weight of the mirror. Ah yes. That damn mirror. Reluctantly, I raised it to my face obscuring the face of the other standing in front of me. Staring back at me was me. Then followed the questions we were encouraged to ask. What does he or she reflect to me about me? Is it possible that this behavior lives within me? When I judge him am I really judging myself, some aspect, some behavior, that he is reflecting to me? Hard questions. Good questions. Necessary questions if you want to truly know yourself—the first step to loving yourself unconditionally.

Naturally, not all of the encounters were reflections of aspects of ourselves that we judged. There were equally as many reflecting what we love about ourselves. We are not only those judged traits. But it is the judged traits that we are looking to reveal to ourselves so that we can find forgiveness and expand the love of self. Forgiveness by my definition.

I realize that this can be a difficult truth to accept. Let me share a personal example. When I first returned to Texas to spend time with my family I quickly became aware that my mother was constantly talking about money, usually the lack or potential lack of it. Every conversation seemed to gravitate back to money. My parents are affluent so there is only a perceived lack rather than an actual lack. It doesn't matter. In fact, it's not about my mother's attitude about money at all. It is about my reaction to her comments, her perceived obsession. My reaction: I was irritated, angry and judgmental. Now, it was not news to me that I have issues around money. This is one of the primary life issues that I am dealing with in this lifetime, along with sexuality of course. There have been periods of my life when I have had lots of money and periods of my life when I have had little. Days when I traveled by private plane and days when I was not sure where I would get the money to feed myself. A roller coaster ride to be sure. Whether I was rich or poor, I was always thinking about money. Once I began receiving the wisdom that I am sharing with you now I began to actively work with the issue.

Each time the money issue came up I would face it consciously. Through my studies I knew that it was not really about the money itself. It was about me and my personal feelings of insecurity and self-worth. It was about trust, trust in life itself. I would read on the subject of money and manifesting. I would meditate and pray. And most importantly, I would become very aware of the feelings that came up for me in the face of poverty or lack. I would feel them without judging them to the degree that was possible for me at the time. I would feel the tightness in my chest and gut. I would breathe deeply and remind myself that, whatever happened, I would not die. I would remind myself that ultimately I am life, and that the life that I AM is eternal. I would face my fears consciously. As I did so, the situation would change, the world around me would transform itself, and the money would begin to flow again. In time.

In my own experience, each time the issue came up my response to it was less dramatic. Each time I gave away less of my peace to this fear. I was making progress by degrees. By the time I returned to Texas I thought I had healed my money issues. My reaction to my mother's comments mirrored the opposite to me. Again, it was not about her. She was simply my mirror, my teacher. My reaction, my judgment of her, was the truth-teller. I was not yet completely healed. I still judged my own money issues. I still feared not having. The test would come again; the opportunity to make peace, the opportunity to choose self-love. And come it did, in spades. I went again from prosperity to poverty. I lost everything and was heavily in debt. My choice was to either blame the economy and the real estate market OR to take responsibility for what I had created in my life and work to change it. Within me. I chose the latter. I used all the tools at my disposal, all that I had learned from my teachers and all that I had learned from living my life consciously. Interestingly enough, although I had little money or income I was living in the guest house on my brother's estate property. My dwelling, though small, overlooked the private pool and gardens. Wisely, I gave thanks for this gift and used it consciously to feed the feeling of prosperity in the midst of the opposite. I reminded myself constantly that this was a good thing, an opportunity for growth and healing. With compassion for self, I persevered. And I triumphed. Once I came to peace with this issue prosperity returned and in greater strength than before. Also, and equally as important, I stopped *hearing* my mother speak about money. Maybe she didn't stop speaking of it but I stopped hearing it. I stopped reacting to it. The world around us is our mirror. The people around us are our mirrors. We only need to look and listen and then bring it back to ourselves. The teachers are already there.

Only you can know what the mirror represents for you. Perhaps it is reflecting a self-judgment. Perhaps it is reflecting an issue that you would be wise to address if you want to be at peace with yourself. Perhaps it is a message that it is time to move on, to move away from the reflections. Only you can know. Sometimes you will only know by taking action and observing the outcome. You must be willing to be honest and truthful with yourself.

I will give you another example. I have a good friend who works in an office environment where there is a lot of drama and anger and chaos. She herself is a peaceful person, not prone to drama. She has also spent decades studying the same wisdom as I have and applying it to her life. She knows herself very well. Why then would her immediate work world be so chaotic, so lacking in peace? Is this a mirror of her own anger and inner chaos that she simply does not acknowledge? Is there something within this chaos, this drama, that somehow serves her in her life? Stimulates her in some way? Is she addicted to it? Or, is this an opportunity for her to experience the chaos and drama and choose to have it be otherwise? To make a profound statement to the Universe that this is enough? To choose a more peaceful, respectful, loving environment in which to work? In other words to make a change in her external world, to manifest a new work situation. Only she can know what the mirror is reflecting. If she feels that it is reflecting a situation in order to move her towards choosing a more appropriate environment and she changes jobs only to find that she is back in a similar situation, then guess what? It's not the situation that needs to change. There is something within herself that she has not yet seen. If she finds her new situation to be one that reflects the peace, love and respect that she feels inside then she has made a powerful I AM statement to the Universe and, chances are, the chaotic work environment will come no more. There are no wrong choices. Each choice can lead to greater wisdom, to greater knowledge and love of self. The key is to be willing to look in the mirror and ask the questions.

I hope this is beginning to make sense to you, to resonate with you. You are the man in the mirror, the woman in the mirror. The mirrors are all around you. If you desire to live in peace with the world around you, first reclaim the peace within you. Peace must begin there. And thank God for that. As a civilization we have proven time and time again that we cannot successfully make peace in the outside world. Not in our homes, our communities, within our country or between our countries. Peace cannot be legislated. It just doesn't work, lastingly. Peace must come from within. From within it influences the without. To reclaim the peace within, you must be willing to discover what takes you away from that place of peace, of balance, of equilibrium. You must be willing to look into the mirrors and see clearly. You must be willing to make peace with what you see. You must use the other tools such as meditation to remind you of this peace, to give you tangible experience of what you might have forgotten, bathing in it whenever you can. We *can* live in a peaceful world. You will notice that as you begin to reclaim your personal peace, the mirrors begin to reflect that peace. Your immediate environment conforms. You find that your environment and the people closest around you are more at peace. As they are influenced by your newly reclaimed state of peace so too are they drawn to rediscover it within themselves. Like a great wave the vibration of peace moves outward from you, the peaceful one. From that sacred place within you the domino effect expands the peace from personal to family to community to state to nation to the world. We *can* live in a peaceful world. In your experience of the world, it can only begin with you, the **Man in the Mirror.**

"Make That . . . . Change . . . ."

CHAPTER X

The Body Human

In the classroom called **SELF LOVE 101** there is yet another great teacher always close at hand and that is your beautiful human body. This body, this miracle of creation, is ever-present and inescapable. It is the unique vehicle that you have consciously chosen within which to re-embark upon this journey, this journey towards peace and unconditional love of self. It is no accident that it is as it is. **As it is** it is the perfect tool for you to uncover and discover what you do not love about you. What you judge. What takes you away from the peace that is yours by right of being.

In the opening sentence above I called your body beautiful. I did so intentionally. What was your reaction to me calling it so? Did you instantly sigh with acknowledgement? Did you bristle with disagreement? Was your first thought, *"Not!"*, or did you smile thinking, *"Yes. I love my beautiful body"*, as you continued to read. Telling signs either way. Your body, the great teacher, the guru. Stop reading right now and contemplate. Ask yourself the question

"How do I feel about my body?"

Grab a piece of blank paper and begin to write:

"My belief about my body is that it is . . . .".

Remember the exercise? Line after line. Let it flow quickly. Do it now!

*   *   *

Welcome back. So, what did you discover or confirm about your thoughts and feelings, your beliefs, surrounding your human body? Any revelations? Any judgments? I suspect so. Few of us are immune. Good. It is with these that you can begin. Chances are good that what you feel about the things that you judge goes much deeper than the superficial. I encourage you to take the courage to look much deeper, to ask the hard questions, and to be truthful with your answers. Once the answer is revealed, ask the question again.

"Is there something more here, something beneath this truth? A deeper truth?"

Go until you feel certain you have exhausted the possibilities, plowed to the depths—of you. Having revealed the answers to yourself, can you now let it all go? Can you forgive? Can you choose to love that part of you that until now you have felt incapable of loving? I know you can. I have journeyed that journey. I grew up with an intense judgment of my physical body and my appearance. I had bad teeth and an overbite. I hated my nose. When I first saw my facial profile in the mirror I was in my teens. I was horrified and so terribly disappointed. I was also thin and without muscles or a well-shaped physique. That is how I saw myself. That is how I judged myself, my body, to be.

By the time I was in my 30's and embarking upon this path toward love of self I felt better about my body and my looks. There were still lingering thoughts about getting my nose fixed but I no longer saw myself as completely unappealing. Now came the time for refinement. While I may not have still judged so harshly I also did not yet love. My body, and my thoughts, feelings, and beliefs about my body, became one of the many tools I was encouraged to use to reclaim peace. I remember standing each morning in the shower consciously scanning my body with my mind. From the top of my head moving down to my feet I would contemplate each body part and speak, *"I love my hair. I love my eyes. I love my ears. I love my nose"*, and so forth. Including my penis which I had long ago deemed to be embarrassingly inadequate in size. Ha! It is true! Did my ego mind argue with me? Sometimes, yes. Loudly so when I would pass by that darned penis. I continued the affirmations. I let the warm water wash over my body and I consciously commanded my love for it, every dang disgusting part of it. In time, the love was truly and honestly felt. The disgust and the judgment were gone.

Why is this even important? That I love my physical body? That I cease to judge any part of it? It is important because we so intensely identify with our bodies. While the higher wisdom is that *"I am not my body"*, most of us do not really know that, feel that. Also, this body is the vehicle of our journey, our transformation. Loving it, as the physical representation of ourselves to the world, is essential to accomplishing the desired goal of loving ourselves completely. **Completely.** The body is tangible. If we can release judgment and find love there then the road to loving those intangible aspects of who we are becomes less rocky. And, when we can feel how good it feels to let go of the judgment of our bodies we are further encouraged to continue down that road.

A few weeks ago as I was moved into a new home I found myself going through boxes from storage, some of which had been put away for many years. Among the many items were old photographs of myself. There were even some from my high school years, those years when I most strongly judged my physical body. My spontaneous reaction was, *"Gosh, Tim, you were actually pretty cute back then!"* It's funny isn't it? Later photos taken in my late 30's when I was studying at the ashram invoked an even more enthusiastic response: *"Wow. What a stud I was then!"* I promise you that, although I had grown to love myself much more completely, I did not feel that way then. Which was true? I was ugly and unattractive in my teens or I was cute? I was fairly attractive in my late 30's or I was a "stud". It is all about perception. Remember that old *Perceiver I*? It is all about my perception of my body, the degree to which I loved it or judged it. So it is true for you. Be wise and take the time to discover your body in a new way, to reveal unto yourself how you really feel about it, and to make your peace with it.

Many teachings about our relationship with our physical bodies will tell you that *"The body does not lie"*. This is an absolute truth. The body does not lie. Think about what I have shared with you about the Law of Attraction and the power of our thoughts, emotions, words, and actions. Consider that all of these are occurring within or through the body. Your physical body, your instrument of expression, literally resonates with the vibrations of these magnetic tones. Imagine the profound effect of that on your beautiful human body. The effect can be miraculously health promoting or it can be devastatingly life destructive. It is up to you. You are the master.

I also spoke to you earlier about what happens when you judge and by doing so block the flow of emotional energy as it moves through your body. Remember the "crimped hose" example? I will say again,

"Emotion is energy in motion"

When an emotion, a feeling, arises from within you, energy moves through the physical body. This movement is resonating at a cellular level within the atomic structure of your cells. When the movement is allowed free flow, the energy, the vibration, brings life giving nourishment to the cells. The atoms respond with an *"I am loved"* attitude. What scientists now call the *God Particle* at the center of the quark within the core of the atom "acknowledges" or "affirms" that the creator of the emotion (that would be you), by allowing the emotion whatever it is, is in alignment with ultimate truth which is that you are <u>love unconditional</u> (God). The wave, the energy of the atom, which is what most of the atom is comprised of, assumes the attributes of *"I am loved"* granted to it by the *Perceiver I* and transmits this quality throughout the cells. Love, life, health of the body, is perpetuated, expanded.

What? I know. I suspect this is a new concept for you and I am not a scientist so my ability to explain it is limited. I am also writing as if your cells and atoms have intelligence and what we call emotion—energy in motion. Again, quantum physics would confirm it to be so. The physicists might use different vocabulary to express the phenomenon but the outcome is the same.

Now, in the example above you have allowed the emotion. No judgment. As a result, life within your body, from the atomic level outward, is nourished. So what happens when you judge the emotion? When you stop the free flow of energy in motion in your body? Again, the *"crimped hose"* effect. An emotion begins to arise from within you. You are not OK with this feeling. Because of conditioning, because of your beliefs, you judge that this is not an OK emotion for you. It is not a good feeling. You suppress the emotion. You stop the flow of energy. You crimp the hose. The message to the cells and the atoms within the cells is clear. I do not like, I do not love, this feeling. This feeling, this emotion, is not OK. It is not good enough to be loved by me. The atoms respond in an *"I am not loved"* attitude. The *God Particle* at the center of the atom notes the mal-alignment with ultimate truth. The energy of mal-alignment commanded by the great creator, you, is acknowledged and then transmitted through the formation and action of the wave. It is seeded within the cellular structure. Dis-ease is born. At the atomic level moving into the cellular. The *God Particle*, because it is a *God Particle* and therefore existing in the state of the unconditional, has no judgment upon what you choose to feel or not feel. In a state of unconditional love everything is OK. Everything is good enough to be God, to be loved. It simply acknowledges your truth and expands it accordingly because the *God Particle* knows, even you do not, that you are the master of your life. You are the god creating things to be as you want them to be.

Your thoughts, words, beliefs and actions also have a contributing effect upon what happens within your body. These further empower your emotional energy and magnify the results. It is, as I have said so many times now, so important to be self-aware, to be aware of your thoughts, words, beliefs and actions and to align them to how you really want to experience your body—and your life.

Already I am hearing your questions in my head.

"OK Tim. I can begin to understand how my blocked or judged emotions can create a disease in the body but what about a newborn baby that is or becomes ill before they are even aware of their emotions?"

This is a great question. First, judged emotions are only one potential cause for disease in the body; one that you can become the master of. We must also consider the effects of karma, of genetics, and of the environment. I have already addressed the subject of karma.

"You reap what you have sown and judged that you have sown".

And remember, the effect of karma is not limited to the sphere of a single lifetime. In that context, remember also that we choose to be born into certain specific situations and conditions, including the state of the human instrument, the body. From the place of choosing we are aware of what conditions and circumstances will best serve us in balancing the karma and in our goal of returning to the conscious state of unconditional love and abiding peace. Such a condition could be a disease, ailment, or imperfection within our physical body.

The science of genetics is now providing us with invaluable information regarding the workings and condition of our bodies. We now know, for example, that there is a genetic propensity toward breast cancer in certain women. And that is only the tip of the iceberg. It is profoundly clear that genetics plays a critical role in the health of our bodies and in our inclinations. Do not forget, however, that, in my world at least, we consciously choose our genetic lineage. We consciously choose our parents. *"Darn it! In Tim's world we never get to play the role of victim!"* You are so right! And, a genetic "propensity toward" does not automatically or necessarily manifest into a cancer or disease. What most influences whether or not a cancer or other disease does manifest out of a genetic propensity toward are our emotions, thoughts, beliefs, words, and actions.

Actions would be what you are doing with and to your beautiful body. How do you treat your body? Do you exercise it consistently and properly? What foods do you eat? What liquids do you drink? Do you smoke? Take drugs? Do you honor it as the magnificent and miraculous temple that it is or do you abuse it or allow it to be abused? Have you educated yourself in nutrition in order to learn what does and does not give nourishment? Do you allow the body its pleasures without judgment? And with respect for it and the bodies of others? Do you give your body sufficient sleep and rest? Do you "pamper" it with deep massages and stimulating baths? Do you oil and lotion it with loving hands?

All of these and many more are actions that send a message to the body. *"I am loved." "I am not loved."* The body *hears* those messages loudly and clearly. The messages sent by the actions taken register deep within the cells, in the atomic structure. That old *God Particle* once again. Remember, the *God Particle* does not judge. It is the unconditional presence of life within all things. As such it merely receives, transmits and magnifies, through the changeable wave within the atom, the message being sent by the God of your bodily kingdom. That, again, would be you. *Your* actions. And those actions that *you* allow to be perpetrated against your body, the temple of your consciousness, your life. If the message received and transmitted is *"I am not loved"* this adds fuel to the fire of mal-alignment, of disease within the body.

Your environment also plays a critical role in maintaining a balance between healthy and unhealthy in your beautiful body. You must be ever-conscious of the world around you and how it might affect your health and well-being. Toxicity comes in many forms, from polluted air to polluted consciousness. An example of polluted consciousness would be hanging around with people who are constantly negative in their thinking and their attitudes. Or people who are violent or harshly judgmental. Or people who do not respect you. Remember, you are influenced by the collective consciousness that surrounds you. I am not judging them. I am categorizing. It is not about making them wrong. It is about choosing what best serves you given what it is you want for yourself.

Your environment. The world you live in. Is there beauty in it? Is it peaceful? Do you feel loved and supported by it?

Do you feel seen and known? Is there too much noise and traffic and drama? Does your environment cause you stress or does it nurture peaceful movement within it? Environment is often the influence that you feel you have the least personal control over. I understand. Can you then alter the manner in which you respond to it? Because again, this environment, the world you live in, and your relationship with it, influences how you feel about you. Given that you are the master and not the victim it also _reflects_ how you feel about you. Read it and then recreate it if does not conform to the vision of who you seek to become.

> *"What if I already have an illness or disease? What if what you have described above has already happened? What can I then do to alter what I have unconsciously created?*

To answer that question we must address the healing of the body and how you, as the master of your life, can participate in that healing.

When I was 39 years old I became aware that I was in the early stages of pancreatic cancer. When I learned of this I was in total shock. I was by this time fairly well along in my studies with my master teacher and living a life that was exciting, expansive, and joyful. Never in my life had I felt more loved—by myself, by those around me, and by my Master who had drawn me into his inner circle. Continuously I was bathed in his love unconditional. *"How could this happen now?"* I cried. *"Now, when I am so happy and feel so deeply loved?"* I was devastated and frightened to my core. The prognosis was that, as it was then seen, the cancer would take my life within six months. It was so damned unfair.

At this same time my Master had embarked with us on the study of a form of shamanism, of healing the body. Non-traditional of course. The approach involved the understandings that I have just shared with you above about the power of emotions, thoughts, words, and actions. It also included ancient Egyptian techniques such as the application of poultices consisting of a specific assortment of powdered crystals and oils. An unorthodox form of body work was also a part of the teachings as was the understanding of chakras and what he called Chakric Consciousness. He and others he had trained began to treat me with these extraordinary methods. I elected not to pursue traditional remedies such as chemotherapy or radiation therapy. In fact I stayed away completely from traditional medicine, in part because I was so immersed in the work with my teacher and our community and in part because the consciousness within the medical community at that time was that pancreatic cancer was incurable. I did not want to be influenced by that particular collective consciousness.

On day one my Master lovingly informed me that, while he would do what he could through these treatments to expel the cancerous cells from my body, he could not heal me of this disease. Only I could do that he said. Keep in mind that already we were deep into the teachings and paramount within those teachings was *"You are the master of your life"*. He counseled me that I, through my unloving thoughts about myself throughout most of my life, had planted the seeds of this disease. Those thoughts of *"I am not loved"*, and the attendant emotions, focused deep in my "gut" and began to slowly squeeze the sweetness of life out of the cells there. The cells of my pancreas.

"You, unconsciously, have created this mal-alignment within your body", he said. *"And only you, you the master of your life, can alter what you have set forth into manifestation. I cannot and will not take this power from you."*

He told me again that he and his students would do what they could to assist in the healing but that the ultimate responsibility was mine.

"Now that the death is beginning to manifest," he advised me, *"you must find from within you a passion for life that is many times more potent that the force of this disease. That will not be easy to do but in that you are the god of your kingdom, you can do it."*

The effect of the applied poultices was immediate. Within hours my body was racked with pain. Severely aching joints, high fever, crushing cramps in my stomach. Already the body was beginning to cast off some of the toxins within the cancerous cells. The liver was taxed by the process and my body became yellow with jaundice. I was so terribly weak that I felt that I could only lay in my bed in suffering. My teacher, with his greater wisdom, demanded otherwise. He insisted that I not only rise from my death bed but also climb with him the many flights of stairs of the hotel in which we were holding the training. In order to win this battle, he said, you must, in every moment, prefer life. However hard it is, you must choose life. In every instance where you give in to the death you empower the movement in that direction.

For months I waged this battle, the battle between life and death. Always my master was there for me, as were my fellow students, some of whom served as shamans to me, all of whom gave me their love and support. Wisely I remained within the community where the consciousness supported the possibility of winning this battle rather than return to my home environment in Texas where the consciousness would be the opposite. Every tool at my command would need to be put to use. Thoughts, emotions, beliefs, actions, environment—all would need to be focused on love of self and passion for life. Every nuance was critical, given the condition of my body. Self-awareness and self-mastery was key.

By this time in our studies we were well aware that death was not something to be feared, that life was ongoing beyond the body. I had not yet fully mastered that truth but I did not so much fear death as I simply did not want this particular life experience to end. As I said earlier, I loved my life. I loved it enough to fight hard for it despite the odds. And I made progress, day by day, week by week, month by month. I could feel it in my body and my master confirmed it.

"The body is healing", he counseled me one evening, *"but the soul is still within the movement toward the dying of this body. You must do what you can to fire up the passion. Go to the ocean that you so love. Play more with the beautiful and life-loving children. Make love.*

Whatever 'gets it up' for you. Do it! Fire up the passion, the passion for life."

Wisely, I followed his advice. One morning, a few weeks later, I awakened to a bright clear day and decided to climb the mountain that rose behind our small settlement. Pleased with my stamina I eventually found myself standing upon a high precipice overlooking the valley below. The wind was battering my body as I leaned out over the precipice. I reveled in the power of it and allowed it to infuse my body and further awaken the power within me. My life force surged within me as I extended my arms and commanded with certainty and unfettered passion,

"I AM LIFE! I AM LIFE! I AM LIFE! I COMMAND FROM THE LORD GOD OF MY BEING I AM LIFE!!!"

The wind calmed as if in confirmation. In that precious moment I knew. I simply knew. The death was vanquished from my body. The cancer was no more. I knew it certainly and without question. Slowly I allowed my body to relax. I sat upon the mountain precipice and I wept. I sobbed my relief and my joy. The battle was won.

A few days later, my master confirmed what I already knew to be true. I was healed. I was 39 years old and I am now 64. Twenty-five years have passed without recurrence. I share my story with you to illustrate and reinforce the wisdom in these pages—how powerful you are when you become conscious and take command of your life. Everything that I have shared with you so far in these reflections had to be consciously applied in the battle for life. Meditation, trust of the inner voice, letting go of judgment, self-awareness, man in the mirror, sexuality, the Law of Attraction—all of it. These were my weapons in the great battle of life over death. Emotion, passion for life, was no doubt the greatest of them but all were pertinent, necessary. And supporting all of these—love of self and the desire for inner peace.

Wow! That was hard. Deep breath Tim. Reflecting upon that challenging period of my life in order that you might benefit from my experience was difficult. While my resolve to share my experiences and what I have learned through them is strengthened, my spirit is momentarily exhausted. I must pause for a moment and give my unsettled soul a brief respite.

*   *   *

Please, please, please, do not wait until you have manifested the illness before you find motivation to apply this wisdom. Your immune system is influenced in every moment by who you are being, what you are thinking, what you are feeling, by all that I have suggested to you. You can assist it in doing its job by living consciously and loving that you live.

As I said above I consciously chose not to go the route of traditional medicine. Do not take that to mean that I am against traditional medicine. While I do find our health industry to be seriously flawed, I do not ignore the great benefits that it offers. The science and technology is phenomenal. And the industry is filled with men and women dedicated to their patients and to the promotion of better health. You would be unwise to dismiss it completely in favor of alternative approaches. The most important thing is to choose an approach with which you feel the most aligned, that resonates with who you know yourself to be. The more clearly you know yourself, the easier this will be to discern. Your beliefs play a critical role. Your faith in the approach you are taking is all-important. All of the wisdom we have discussed above can be, should be, applied, whatever the approach taken. If you are choosing radiation therapy or surgery for example, these will only increase your chances of a successful outcome. Meditation is proven to assist in managing pain and enhancing healing. Take the time to consider your beliefs and those of the people closest around you that will be supporting you in your healing process. Be truthful with yourself. Know yourself. And then love yourself enough to utilize the healing approach that is most likely to bring you what you want.

Healthy or sick, you should always be aware of the influence of social consciousness and conditioning. In the United States we are inundated in the media with advertisements on this disease and that ailment. Usually these influences are fear based. They are designed to cause fear to rise within you so that you will seek out their proposed drug or treatment. Remember what I have said about the power of fear within the scope of the Law of Attraction? Do your best to avoid these negative influences.

There is an entire consciousness around illness and disease that, in my opinion, needs to shift if we are to succeed in living healthier, happier lives. There is too great a focus on being unwell rather than on being well. Ours is not so much a health industry as it is an illness industry. And our illnesses too readily become banners with which we define ourselves. This is true in the very simplest of ways. How often, for example, do you find yourself saying, *"I am sick"*? *"Well, Tim, only when I am sick!"* I hear you. But think about it. Given all of the wisdom that I have shared with you what effect do you think that has on your status? *"I am sick." "I have this disease". "I have that ailment."* I know that it feels as though you are only stating the truth. But in reality you are forcefully claiming the disease as your own. We must learn to change our vocabulary. Get creative. Find a more positive way to express what is happening, to explain our situation. We must consciously shift to using our thoughts and words to affirm what we really want our experience to be. I grant you that this is not easy. I wrestle with it myself. Given what I have learned from my own experience I also know that it can make a huge difference in keeping our beautiful bodies healthy and vibrant with life.

*   *   *

I realize that this has become a long chapter but there is simply so much to consider when we talk about the body human and its role in our journey to reclaim personal peace and rediscover unconditional love of self. There is but one more tool that I want to address and that is related to our earlier discussion of meditation. I spoke to you about meditation as a valuable and necessary tool to reintroduce you to the peace that you are seeking and to give you more ready access to your inner wisdom. Meditation is also a valuable tool in maintaining and improving the health of your physical body. This is not mere speculation. I quote a posting by Family Health Guide on their website:

"In the words of Dr. Herbert Benson, who led the (meditation) research group at the Harvard Medical School, 'We found a range of disease fighting genes that were active in the relaxation practitioners but not active in the control group'. In as little as two months after the control group began meditating, their genetic profile changed to resemble those of the relaxation practitioners. Several other studies designed specifically to understand the benefits of meditation have shown variously that meditation helps to reverse heart disease, reduce pain, lessen chronological aging, reduce blood pressure, fight inflammation, decrease anxiety, and control asthma."

So, it is not just Tim and the gurus telling you to meditate. If your purpose in life is to reclaim personal peace and rediscover unconditional love of self, meditation can guide you down that path. As you are traveling your journey it can also assist you to maintain your beautiful body, the vehicle that transports you on your journey, in a condition that will best serve you to achieve the fulfillment of your purpose.

Guided visualization meditations are also a very effective tool for self-healing and are available from countless sources in CD, DVD, and MP3 formats. Many can also be found as YouTube videos. These incorporate imagery into the meditative experience to evoke healing, relieve stress, and create a passageway into your personal place of peace. I, myself, offer guided meditative experiences which I call **Conscious Creator Imagery**. My approach is based upon the understanding that you are the creator of your life, consciously or unconsciously. Utilizing the rhythm and tone of my voice I lovingly guide you into that place of peace we have spoken of, that place of inner wisdom, of divine presence. From that place of *Creator Power* I guide you with very specific imagery to focus upon whatever issue or illness that you are looking to address. For example, If are you seeking to heal from lung cancer the imagery is directed to the lungs and is designed to utilize the power of sound, imagination and consciousness to affect an alteration at the cellular and atomic level. As I guide you through the experience I myself go to that place of *Creator Power* and become for you another powerful *Perceiver I*, envisioning with you, creating with you, the desired outcome. You can learn more about **Conscious Creator Imagery** and find guided meditation downloads on my website: www.timothyernster.com.

CHAPTER XI

The Breath of Life

About 10 years ago, while in Israel to participate in an International Conference on Forgiveness, I found myself seated in the beautiful and ancient church at the Benedictine monastery at Abu Gosh. Resident monks were reverently chanting a hymn in Latin, the deep resonant tones creating an atmosphere sacred and solemn. Enjoying the sweet peace of my surroundings I slowly slipped into a deep state of transcendence. Suddenly, and unexpectedly, all the voices around me were transmuted into one sound and that sound became the words, "One Breath". "One Breath" became a repeating mantra that penetrated my being. "One Breath, Timothy. We are One Breath". A veil of ignorance lifted in my consciousness and all things became clear.

We are One Breath. No separation. The breath that lives me lives all. It is the breath of life. It is there that we are ONE. In the breath, the one breath that lives each of us, regardless of faith, or culture, or country. Regardless of age, or sex, or color, or consciousness. We are One. One Breath. One Life.

It was so simple, so obvious in a sense. And yet, in that moment it was a revelation. As I left the church I walked in the garden remembering my Master's teaching on how and when the soul enters into the body. He told us that the soul, your soul, my soul, all souls, comes and goes from the fetus during the pregnancy. As if it is testing the waters, visiting the new house. The point at which the soul becomes firmly seated in the body, in the new incarnation, is with the intake of the first breath. It is the breath that carries the soul into the body to be seated there. One breath and you are in. One Breath. And when and how does the soul depart the body ending the incarnation? You guessed it. With the final breath. One breath and you are out. One Breath. You, your consciousness, your divine Self, housed within the soul, rides within this breath that all of us share, that we all have in common. This One Breath.

"So, lovely Tim, but why are you telling me this? What does this have to do with loving myself unconditionally?"

For me, in that moment of realization, it was yet another confirmation that we are all One. That it is not just spiritual poetry. That we are not separate from one another. We share this one breath.

The sense of separation, of aloneness, is one of the many "feelings" that keep us from loving ourselves and our fellow humans unconditionally. And again, our conditioning tends to reinforce this belief in separateness. Our physical senses seem to confirm it. I am alone. I am separate from those around me, even from those with whom I am the most intimate, emotionally, sexually, romantically. *"I am alone"* equates in our conditioned minds to *"I am not loved"*. *"I am not loved"* equates to *"I am not worth loving"*. If I feel that I am not worth loving then it is very hard for me to love myself unconditionally. That is why I think that the concept of One Breath is so important. It is yet another way to see yourself as NOT separate, as NOT alone, as NOT unloved. It is another way to expand the unconditional love of self.

I have stated in an earlier chapter that quantum physics has confirmed this to be true—that we are not alone. That we are all interconnected within the apparent space that seems to separate us by atomic stringlets and that we exist within a great and endless unseen web of atomic connectedness. Remember that the atom itself is mostly space, more wave than particle. The soul, which you do not see with your human eyes, is known to have weight and mass. It weighs a measurable 13 ounces. This can be calculated if you weigh the body before and immediately after the soul passes. That you do not see it does not mean that it does not exist. More wave than particle remember. More "spirit" than "matter". It is mostly what we think of as vibration, as energy, and vibrating at a faster rate of speed than the cells that make up your body, your body that you can see. So too the breath. Unless your breath is laden with moisture you do not see it. Does it then not exist? Are you breathing my friend? If you are reading this we can assume that you are. And where, pray tell, does your breath go to when it leaves your body? And where does the next intake of breath come from? Hmmmmm.

And what exactly *is* this breath that you are breathing? That your life depends upon? We readily accept that it is necessary to sustain life but do we know what it is exactly.

"Well, oxygen Tim! And carbon dioxide! It is air Tim!"

Do carbon and oxygen have atomic structure?

"Well, of course, Tim!

Ahhh. So this breath that lives you, this breath that we all share, is atomic in structure? And within the quark at the center of these atoms that the One Breath is made of exists what has become known as the God Particle? The same God Particle that exists within the atoms that make up my physical body? That make up my soul? Interesting. And this breath that lives the body, that is the air that we breath, the life that lives us, is essentially only One Breath shared by all of us, existing in the space that seems to separate us? Now that IS interesting. The space that SEEMS to separate us. The God Particle exists within that space that seems to separate us? That space from which we draw our breath, into which we expel our breath? That infinite space where we are one breath, one life? ONE.

I am playing with you a bit in order to make my point:

You are not alone.

You are loved unconditionally by that which sustains your life. We are connected to one another at our very essence by that which fuels the life that we live. The breath. And it is the state of Unconditional Love, residing within the God particle, that permits and sustains this connectedness, that grants validity to the poetic statement: WE ARE ONE. The more you are able to see this, to accept this as truth, the more you are able to grow in unconditional love of self. I believe that, if we are wise, we use every tool available to us to get there, to know and feel this love. It is for this reason, and this reason alone, that I present to you the concept of One Breath. I implore you to consider it.

*   *   *

The breath. We all breathe, right? We take it for granted. It is natural, habitual, unconscious. Unless of course we have a breathing disorder. Then we become very conscious breathers. Every breath is a miracle. But for most of us breathing is an unconscious act, a force of habit. The body breathes. It is as simple as that. Most of us pay little attention to it. I am now going to suggest that you do pay attention to it, your breath. I am going to suggest that you take time during the day to stop whatever you are doing and become aware of your breath. Several times a day. Become aware of the ebb and flow, the movement, of your breath. How deep are you breathing? Only to the chest? Deep into the abdomen? The ideal is to breathe deeply, to allow the abdomen to fill with air in a natural movement. Not forced, but full. Nice and easy. You want the entirety of your body to benefit from the flow of oxygen, the breath of life.

You remember our discussion about chakras? You want to imagine that the breath moves all the way down to the root chakra, to the base of your spine, to the perineum. The perineum is located between the anus and the testicles or vagina. That should be the image—the breath fills the abdomen and touches the perineum before rising again up the body. Stop right now and check the movement of your breath. To where does it move in the body? Is the movement easy or forced. Become aware.

Awareness is key. Consciousness is critical. The breath brings oxygen into your body whether you are breathing consciously or habitually. Thank God! However, if you add awareness into the mix the effect of the breath is magnified. Remember the Perceiver I? Awareness of, attention to, alters the condition of. This goes back to the "observer effect" in quantum physics. The quality, the behavior, of the atom is altered by the observation of it. By the simple act of you paying attention to it, it is altered.

Now, consider this. Suppose the awareness, the consciousness, that you place upon the breath is:

"I am life. I am love. I am health. With each breath my body becomes more alive, more healthy, more happy. With each breath I become more certain that I am loved unconditionally."

What might the effect be? Right. The breath will carry more strength, health, vitality, life, and dare I say it, unconditional love into your precious body. Hallelujah!!!

If you are practicing the meditations I recommended then you are already taking some time to breathe consciously. Good for you. In my studies with my Master we also practiced pranayama breath which is a specific technique which induces the presence of prana or life force into the body. Pranayama breath has been a staple of sacred mystical practices throughout the ages. It is a more sophisticated approach that the one I have just suggested to you, involving various methods of taking the breath in and out. For the mystics, they are consciously breathing God, Divine Light, into their bodies. For you, and for this course in Self Love, it is sufficient to perceive it as breathing in life, health, vitality, and most importantly, unconditional love.

The healing power of the breath, of bringing more oxygen into the body, is not simply something the mystics agree on. Even the most "old school" of physicians will tell you the same thing in different words.

"Oxygenate the body!"

Recent studies have indicated, if not proven, that cancer cells cannot survive in a highly oxygenated environment. Scientists, physicians, metaphysicians, and mystics may not all agree with that but they do all agree that breathing deeply, breathing life-giving oxygen into the body, is essential to good physical, mental, emotional and spiritual health. I and the mystics further concur that breathing consciously magnifies the positive effects.

So breathe baby breathe
Breathe deeply
Breathe consciously

* * *

These past few weeks, in the midst of writing this book, I personally took my awareness of the power of the breath to a new level. I had long been aware of the various approaches to utilizing conscious breath work for personal transformation— for healing the body, releasing blocked emotions, and creating a more open flow of energy. In other words, to create a happier, more healthy and productive life experience. I was aware of them peripherally but had not employed them nor was I drawn to do so. For many months, though, I had been dealing with several physical health issues, all in the root chakra and naval chakra areas of my body. I was also having trouble moving energy out into the world, creating in the world, and making decisions in that regard. I prayed daily for guidance as to how to best heal the body and how to move the stuck energy.

As is often the case the answer came in a most unexpected fashion. A new friend that I had met online had invited me to spend a week at his home on the island of Lanzarote in the Canary Islands. I was at that point planning another return to France and so agreed to make that my first stop. I knew, of course, that my friend was a facilitator of Transformational Breath Work. We had discussed his work often online. But, in my mind, I was going to Lanzarote for a holiday, not therapy. Right. Of course, once I arrived and settled in, he offered to introduce me to the breath work. I agreed and thus commenced an amazing journey for me.

How hard can it be, right? Breathing. Right. To begin, he simply observed my normal breathing pattern. Just as I have asked you to do with yourself. Told me that I wasn't breathing fully into my body, deep into my root chakra. Me, a meditator! A practitioner of conscious breath! I bit my tongue and observed along with him. He was right! Darn it! Told me that I wasn't grounded in my body, rooted in the earth. Me? A real estate guy from Texas. How much more grounded do you want? He then told me that all of these health issues in the pelvic and abdominal region of my body were related to that. That the breath was not reaching this area of my body and the energy there was blocked resulting in assorted chronic physical problems. My body and my energy centers were out of balance. Whoa! And that, furthermore, my inability to make decisions about my life, to move creative energy out into the world, was also related directly to this lack of being grounded, this blocked energy, this imbalance. In effect, this area of my body was starving for life, for the breath of life.

From that day on we did a breath work session each day for the week that I was there. We also breathed and meditated together in the early morning. During a session you are in a specific posture and breathe in specific manner. While you are breathing the facilitator works meridian points on the body to release blocked energy and permit the breath to permeate and do its thing. It is not easy, sometimes painful. Lots of "stuff" can come up. The facilitator is there to move you through it. Mine was brilliant at it. No accident that he is known as the Breath Guru. Because of the positive influence of this type of breath work, the body can experience a form of detoxification. That is a nice way of saying that you might feel worse before you feel better. I certainly did. Fortunately, my friend and therapist was always there to support and encourage. He also fueled my body with healthy shakes and green drinks to further facilitate the healing process.

It was the following week when I was visiting friends in Paris that the positive effects of the work became apparent to me. The health issues of my lower body all but disappeared. I was invigorated and more decisive. My sexual energy came alive again. Opportunities began to appear regarding my work in the world. Feeding humanity, remember? So pleased was I with the results that I scheduled a return to Lanzarote for another week of intensive breath work complimented by body work to be then followed by a week by the sea writing and relaxing. I am there now enjoying the writing and relaxing part. Again, the work was hard. And again the results were profound.

I share this story with you to further emphasize the power and importance of the breath. I also share it with you to remind you that this journey, this path of self love, is unending. There is always room for refinement. More to know of oneself. More conditions to move beyond. Moving farther into the unconditional. It also serves as a reminder that our prayers, our conscious intentions, are responded to. By a loving Universe that we are the co-creators of. Often, deeply immersed in ego, we fail to hear or see the response. I was fortunate. My higher self used the ego self to get me where I needed to be—on a magical island that offered transformation and a holiday of sun and sea. And into the hands of a master of the breath. I am grateful to those in body and those in spirit who pushed and pulled me in the right direction.

Breathe

CHAPTER XII

Attachment and the Fear of Death

It is an awesomely beautiful day back here in my little haven on the Texas coast. I gaze out the window to witness several deer with their yearlings silently grazing amongst the oaks. A scattering of ducks glide gracefully across a pond. The sun is bright and warm on this late January day as a light breeze blows in from the bay bringing the sweet scent of salty air. It is so tranquil and so very peaceful. I am truly blessed.

Yes, I am blessed. I also worked very hard and very diligently to manifest this peace, this tranquility. This that I view from my window is, for me, the ready reflection of what I have gained in my long and adventurous journey, what my master calls *"The Journey Home"*. It is the ready reflection of that which now exists as an abiding presence within me. Peace. As I look upon this confirming reflection I think of you, you whom I seek to guide along your own path, your own *Journey Home.* In these pages I have attempted to share with you what I have learned along the way, to provide you with tools to empower you on your journey, and to tell some of my own story in order to inspire and to confirm the validity of what I offer. Some, I know, you will take to heart and implement in your lives. Some you will discard as simply not the truth for you or not applicable in your individual experience. This is as it should be. **You are the master of your life**. I am, hopefully, a light in the window to guide you steadily back to you. No more can I ask.

On this great journey home there is yet another mountain to conquer in order to reach the journey's end and that is the great mountain called **Attachment**. It is not only the teaching of all great sages but it also the meat of my own experience:

"You cannot know pure peace if you are attached to anything or anyone."

And we, as humans, when we begin this journey, are attached to damn near everything. That is my observation and my experience. We are attached to things, to people, to places, to ideas, to identities, to life itself. We are attached. We are owned by the things that we own. We are possessed by the people we love. We hold fast to ideas and opinions as if our lives depend upon them. Our identities are sacrosanct. We hold on to them for fear that without them we are nothing, no one. We are attached.

To the degree that we are attached the stability of our equilibrium is threatened. That state of centeredness, of knowing you are loved, of peace, if dependent upon that or they that surround us, is vulnerable to upset. We can be pulled off center by a change in circumstance. We can be pulled off center if a person's attitude or opinion towards us shifts even slightly. We can be pulled off center if how we are experienced professionally is suddenly altered somehow. If we lose a loved one. If even the threat of that happening appears. If what we always thought was true now appears to be untrue. If our own lives are threatened in some way. Or our livelihood. To live at the mercy of the ebb and flow of these circumstances, these life occurrences, is to live without peace.

Most of us live our lives somewhere along a spectrum of peaceful centeredness. We can remain relatively at peace if confronted by new ideas. We are confident about our ability to manifest financially so we do not feel threatened if our financial circumstances change. Our peace-stealing anger over a wrecked car that we loved passes quickly. The loss of our beautiful home takes months to reconcile. We are slightly disturbed from our state of peaceful centeredness if our health is threatened but much more so if the health of our child is threatened. We are devastated if that child's life is taken or the life of a spouse or partner or other loved one. Our pain is so great that we abandon entirely our otherwise fairly stable state of peaceful equilibrium, at least for a time. For many the state of true peace never returns in that lifetime, so great is the pain or anger or guilt or despair.

I do not have children or a spouse in this lifetime so my ability to remain at peace in the face of such a loss is purely speculative, and doubtful. I *have* lost a beautiful home, a thriving business and the identity attached to that business. I have experienced having my life threatened by a deadly cancer. I have encountered the loss of my wealth. I have lost to untimely deaths friends that I have loved and I have most certainly seen my ideas and beliefs questioned to the extreme. To what degree did I remain at peace in the face of these experiences?

Mmmmm. I find myself smiling in contemplation of my response. The road to mastery has been a long one. In the early miles along that road my ability to even *find* peace was limited, my ability to hold on to it in the face of the above noted incidences even more so. We are all, myself included, masters in progress. In some cases I was assisted and supported by a wise teacher and loving friends. In others, I was left only to myself and had to draw upon the resources that I had accumulated by living a conscious life dedicated to knowing this peace and love. Now, in my 64th year, while pleased with my progress I can't say with certainly that the peace boat cannot be rocked. Time will tell.

When I speak about not being attached I am not speaking about renunciation. I am not speaking about giving up the things of this world, nor the people in it. I am not suggesting that you let it all go and head up to a cave in the mountains to live in isolation so that you might find peace. No. This, I can fairly safely say, is not your path. It is a path that few are destined to walk and those that are so destined are typically not born into Western culture. Your path, like my own, is about learning to live in the midst of the material world, in the presence of human relationships, fully engaged in life, and still maintain a steady and centered peacefulness at your core. That is not an easy path to walk.

It is a conundrum at best. In order to not be attached, to remain at peace in the face of anything, you must love yourself unconditionally. Conversely, in order to love yourself unconditionally you must not be attached to anything. Which comes first, the chicken or the egg? In this case they join each other on the path and walk the road together. Sometimes the chicken walks ahead, sometimes the egg. You must start the journey with an honest assessment of where you are now. Remember "Know Thyself"? For most of us, as we embark upon the road, the path, there are a certain amount of conditions that we have placed upon how we love ourselves. Likewise, there is a certain amount of attachment to things, ideas, identities, persons. We are perfectly imperfect. I am attached to certain things and to others I am not. I am attached to only this person but not to others. I love these aspects of myself but not those. I love that I am generous but I do not love my physical body. We are perfectly imperfect.

In order to make the imperfect perfect we want to draw upon the love of self that *is* there to support us in the letting go of our attachment to a specific something or someone. An example: I love the generosity that I am. *And* I would like to release my attachment to having my beautiful home. Good. What are the feelings that arise within you when you think about losing your beautiful home? Anger? Resentment? If you go deeper in search of the core emotion you will find that it is fear, and at the very deepest level, fear of death. *"I feel that I will die if I lose my home"*. The feeling is that strong. That is the basis for your attachment. You are emotionally attached to having your beautiful home because you fear that you will die without it. That may initially seem like an exaggeration to you. I hear you.

"No, Tim, I do not feel that I will die. I will just be extremely disturbed and angry. I will be disturbed that I cannot create another one as beautiful. I am afraid that I might even become homeless. Where will I live?"

OK. Good enough. Already these emotions have been sufficient to rob you of your peace. They have pulled you off balance, out of equilibrium with yourself. You are, by definition, attached to your home. In effect, your home owns you and not the reverse. It is not the home that is the issue. It is your emotional attachment to it that is the issue. Your goal should be to be able to keep your home and keep your peace. How to begin? "**I love the generosity that I am**." You begin with that. Focus your awareness on that for a moment. Feel the love that you feel for the generous person that you are. Let the feeling of love of this aspect of who you are grow and blossom within you. You are conscious that you love this aspect of who you are unconditionally. No judgment. Good. Now, return to the thought of losing your beautiful home. Go there in your mind. Let the emotions resurface. The anger. The resentment. The fear. Whatever comes that robs you of your peace. Now, in your mind, your imagination, you begin to envision bathing the fearful feelings in a soft white light, the light of the love that you feel for your generous self. Like a soothing balm the loving light begins to soften the fearful emotions. You begin to move from feeling disturbed to being at peace. Your repetitive thoughts are:

"I am loved. I am loved. I am loved.
Whatever happens, I am loved.
I draw from the love I am to expand the love I am.
I am loved.
I live. I live. I live.
The life that I am is of me.
The life that I am is ongoing into forever.
Nothing outside of me can take this life that I am.
I am life. I am love. I am peace.
So Be It!"

Allow these thoughts and feelings to settle into your being, to be absorbed by your body, mind and consciousness. Breathe.

After a few moments return your thoughts to your beautiful home and the potential loss of that home. What are you now feeling? Chances are good that there is less anger, resentment, fear. You are, at the very least, a little more at peace with the thought, less disturbed by it. Your attachment is diminished. You have taken another step along your path to personal peace and unconditional love of self. We are all masters in progress. Every step is an important one. Play the game of imagining the loss again and again over time. In time the fear will be gone.

This is a great technique for releasing attachment without requiring the actual loss of the home in order for you to pay attention to your attachment and let it go. Either journey will get you the same desired results. I required the actual loss. This I do not recommend. It did work. I gained the wisdom of detachment, of not being attached. Love was expanded and peace was restored. But it was a hard lesson. What I am hoping to do here is to you guide around such necessities. It is important to note here that you cannot have it both ways. If you declare to the Universe, *"I want pure and abiding peace and unconditional love of self"*, do not be surprised when the Universe sends you the opportunities to get exactly what you called out for. Attachment keeps you from knowing that peace and therefore must be addressed one way or the other.

The beautiful home is just one example I could have used to illustrate. It is also one that I have lived personally. The most challenging of our attachments to make peace with are naturally our attachments to those we love. If we think of our lover, our spouse, our children, our parents, our siblings, we tend to feel that being attached to them being there, being happy, being healthy, being safe, is right and good. Loving them *is* right and good. Being attached is not. This is a hard one I know. And I cannot claim to have mastered it. I have not had in my life that one great love. I do not have children. I do have parents and siblings and feel that I have released my attachment to them. I have not yet been tested. Needless to say, these are not the attachments you begin with as you embark upon your journey. They are best addressed as you grow stronger in self-love and your personal peace is more firmly established within you. However, life does not always follow the rules. You might tomorrow be faced with a situation that tests the strength of your attachment to someone you love deeply. I pray not. Would that I could have utilized my imagination to engage with my attachment to my physical life rather than requiring that an actual cancer manifest to threaten it. I did not. I am the most stubborn of students. I have often needed "bricks upon my head" in order to get me to change. The outcome has been good but I do not recommend the procedure.

In the example I used above I proposed that the core emotion supporting the attachment was fear of death. This is the fear beneath all fears. It lurks beneath most of our attachments and is the single most powerful cause of imbalance, of the absence of peace, in our lives. The fear of death. Those of us who are Christians speak often of heaven, of meeting with God or Jesus when we die, of being reunited with our loved ones, of "eternal peace". And yet, very few of us really want to go there. *"Yes, someday, but please not today".* Our society encourages us to do anything possible in order to delay death. Quality of life is readily sacrificed on the sacred altar of mortality. So, do we really believe that heaven awaits us? And if so, why the resistance? Why the fear? Yes, there is the pleasure and enjoyment of our present life, the presence of those we love, the adventure. This I understand. I am not suggesting that we should rush headlong into our inevitable deaths. Not at all. This human life is a great gift, a grand opportunity.

I do suggest that we would be well served by taking the time to contemplate death and our thoughts and fears surrounding death. You would be wise to contemplate *your* death and how you feel when you think about it. If today was your last day in this body, what would be your regrets? Is there something that you will wish you had said or done? Would you greet your departure with fear? Would your last goodbye be spoken with a smile of peace-filled awareness?

Fear of the unknown fuels the fear of death. What are your beliefs about life after death? What is your conditioning? Love yourself enough to educate yourself, to expand what you now know to be the possibilities. Pursue the ideas that I have postulated in this book regarding the ongoingness of life. Of lives past and future. Of the "heavenly" interludes. Your fear of death can be tempered by knowledge, by making the unknown more known. I suppose that we can never know completely until we have again made the passage. I only know what feels true for me. What I have come to know, to believe, has nourished my state of inner peace. It feels true for me. It makes sense to me. I am comforted and I do not feel afraid when I contemplate my eventual passing. That might change when I am staring death in the face. Who can be certain?

The work I have done on my path has certainly prepared me. I have left no words unspoken to those whom I love. There are no strong judgments that I still hold on myself. There are no major dreams unfulfilled. There is no one and no thing that I am so attached to that I would hold on to human life at all costs. These are the things that make this life and the life after "hell". The words unspoken. The dreams unfulfilled. The judgments of oneself. The regrets. And these you take with you to some degree as you pass on. Death does not wipe the slate clean. It is simply a doorway. The *you* that steps through that doorway is the *you* that arrives on the other side. Darn it!

Best to make your peace now, to do the work now, to let go the attachments, including the attachment to this physical life, now, to allow the love now. If you fear that you will be punished for the perceived wrongs that you have perpetrated, then make amends now. Find forgiveness now (by my definition of forgiveness which is loving acceptance without conditions). Remember, fear is a very powerful manifesting emotion, the most powerful. You do not want fear to be the ruling emotion as you approach your passing. What do you think that will create for you beyond the doorway? Peace? Or the experience of exactly what it is that you fear most strongly? This is my definition of hell. Your life, the life that lives you, does not end at the doorway. The Law of Attraction is a Universal Law. It is not limited to the realms of the physical. Love yourself unconditionally in this lifetime, in this body human. Reclaim your peace in this lifetime. Then, as you approach the doorway of death, you can know that this is what awaits you on the other side—all-consuming peace and love unconditional.

Hmmm. That sounds a lot like what some of us call Heaven, doesn't it!

CHAPTER XIII

Living Your Goodness

In an earlier chapter I spoke to you about the concept of "acting as if" or "wearing the coat of". If you wish to become something or someone different you begin to act as if you already are that something or someone. If you want to become a successful businessperson, for example, you start to act like your vision of someone who is a successful businessperson. You wear the coat of the successful businessperson. Yes, you pretend. Remember pretending? You were so very good at it as a child. How would a successful businessperson speak? How would she dress? Who would he likely be associating with? In what kinds of places would she spend her free time? Who do you know that is already living this experience, someone that is already successful? Call them up and ask them to dinner. When you sit with them, feel their essence, the qualities they exhibit that speak to you of their success. Take what feels appropriate for you and weave it into your coat of many colors—the coat of the successful businessperson.

It is the feeling that is important. You want to use all of these tools in order to feel what it feels like to be what you wish to become. All of the pretending is just to assist you into the emotion. The power to manifest lies in the emotion. Remember? Once you get the feeling of what it is you want to become, you nurture it. Again, using the pretending talents you have owned since childhood. Soon, inside of you, you are this successful businessperson. You have only now to take appropriate right action to cause the physical reality to match the emotional reality. The Law of Attraction will propel you. You, of course, must also have prepared yourself in the physical realm to assume this new identity. By that I mean the studies, the work experience, the mentoring, and the due diligence. If you skip that part and simply "wear the coat" emotionally, the coat in physical reality will likely be too large for you and you will only be disappointed. This is a form of self-sabotage. You are wiser than that.

I use the example of businessperson as one of a multitude of possibilities. I also use it to lead us into another important application of this approach to self-creation and that is in regards to living your goodness. I remind you that the goal of this path along which I am guiding you is to reclaim personal peace and attain unconditional love for yourself. Most of us love what is good; what we, as humans, as a society, deem to be good. We still live in a world of duality—good and bad, light and dark, love and hate. The masters, saints, and sages will tell us that this sense of duality is an illusion, that the higher truth is that everything simply IS; that in the eyes of God, everything is perfect as it is. It sounds so beautiful doesn't it? And I, for one, believe it is true. However, I do not live there. Not yet. And neither do you. That is the world in which I dream to live. It is not the world in which I live today.

In my desire to someday live as the masters live, I wisely "wear the coat" of a master as often as I can. I draw from what I know of masters such as Jesus and Buddha and of the many lesser known but equally adept. Although I have become familiar with other masters through my studies, and certainly use my own spiritual Master as an example, Jesus is the master I grew up with. The stories from my Catholic childhood still resonate. And those that resonate most clearly are the stories of his goodness. His kindness. His acts of giving, of loving. His entire being was one of unconditional love. This was his vibration and this was visible in his actions. This is what I seek to become. This is the dream to be realized, the prize of my path. It only makes sense to me that if I can emulate him, and others like him, this can speed me on my way.

Suffice it to say that I am not quite ready to emulate resurrection and raising the dead. I can, however, emulate his goodness, emulate their goodness. I can put on the coat of one who is good, one whose acts demonstrate his love for humanity, even when his love for humanity is not evident even to himself. That is *my* love for humanity I am speaking about. I may not be there yet but I can act as if. Acting as if is not a lie. Deep within me I do love humanity. The pain and conditioning has masked this love. I am simply reaching out to find that deep truth, to remove the mask. By doing so, I become aware that when I wear the coat of goodness, when I act as if I am a loving and giving person, I feel more love towards myself.

Let me say that again.

When I act as if I am a loving and giving person, I feel more love towards myself.

I grow in my love of myself. Acts of goodness expand love of self. I feel better about myself. I feel good. I feel love. I feel more loving towards me. Yes, this is a result of my conditioning. I am conditioned to believe that acts of goodness render me more worthy to be loved. Being aware of that, I then use my conditioning to expand my love of self. Pretty smart of me, huh? What is really great about this is that because I feel more loving towards myself when I am kind to another I am then motivated to be kind more often. As I am more kind, love of self expands. The selfless act becomes a self-serving act. Why not!

And it is so easy really. Of all of the tools and techniques that I have shared with you in this book, none are as easy as this. Looking the check-out lady in the eyes and asking her if she is having a good day? Holding the door open as a man approaches? Saying good day to a neighbor? Complimenting a friend's pretty sweater? Smiling at those you pass on the street? This is not hard work. Simple acts of goodness, of kindness. You don't have to spend the day feeding the poor and hungry although this will certainly expand your love of self immensely. Do what you can. There is a lot you can do as you go about your day. Simple acts of kindness. Living your goodness. Acting "as if" in those moments when you don't actually feel it. Noting how good it feels; how acting "as if" uplifts you as well as the other.

The goodness that you feel will seek more of itself. Law of Attraction. More acts of kindness will come your way, confirming to your human consciousness that you are indeed good and worth loving. You have created a movement, a circle of goodness and love. At the center of that circle you will begin to find peace, to *know* peace. And power. The power of the love that you are. The power to expand that love.

Unconditional love is born out of the conditional. If you must begin with the condition, *"I feel love for myself because I did a good thing"*, so be it. Let that be the beginning place. If the condition is that you have to "pretend" to want to do the good thing, so be it. The love born out of these conditions will expand naturally. Soon enough you will not need to pretend. Soon enough the love that you feel for yourself because you *did something good* becomes simply the love you feel for yourself. It is there without requirements to make it so. You love yourself not *because of* but simply *because*. You are. No conditions. Unconditional. Love.

Wear the coat, the coat of your goodness. Let it enfold you and comfort you. Let it warm you on your journey with the love that you are. It is true. You are this love. One day you will stand empowered and let the coat drop from your shoulders. You will need it no more. You will have become what you have dreamed to become, what you have pretended to be, living the goodness that you are.

CHAPTER XIV

At Long Last . . . . Love

Last chapter. Final suggestion. I want you to take some time to find your own quiet place where you are free to reflect, to contemplate. Once you have found this space, I ask that you lay before you the wisdom, techniques, philosophies, and contemplations that I have shared with you through my own reflections. Lay before you perhaps the Table of Contents that lists the chapter titles of this book. Gaze upon it to remind yourself of what we have covered here. Read each heading and sit with it long enough to let the mind remember some of what was written and the soul to recall that which resonated most deeply for you. Once done, lift your eyes and gaze as through a window into and onto your own life, taking with you as you do so the thoughts of the subjects listed.

As you gaze in contemplation into and unto your life ask yourself the questions:

"What is it I seek most to attain through this life that I am living?"

"Are abiding peace and unconditional love of self MY goals?"

"Do I now claim these as my ultimate life purpose, riding above and beyond, and yet alongside, the other human goals?"

You, and only you, can answer these questions. My goals may not be your goals. My path may not be your path. If you have stuck with me this far it is likely that we are in some degree of accord. Perhaps you are only curious. Only you can know. Trust what you feel.

Contemplate the questions and allow the answer to rise to the surface of your consciousness. They will come. Look back upon your life. Consider what you have lived. Consider what you wish to create. Reflect. Do not judge what you remember, what you have done. Simply reflect upon it. Do not judge what you dream to create. Simply reflect upon it. Envision it. I have my personal vision of what we have come into this life to accomplish, to realize—the purpose of our very human lives. I have shared with you this vision and what I know has assisted me to achieve it, to the level that I have achieved it. You can claim it as your own but it must feel true for you. It must feel right. If it does then you have set yourself upon the ready road, a path is laid out for you. This path is a guide. SELF LOVE 101. It is broad and not narrow. You can adapt it to your own truths. You can massage it to fit your situation. You can flavor it with the flavor of YOU.

You are the Master of Your Life

Let us now review together those issues that I feel to be the essentials on this particular path to peace and love, those that I have presented to you in the preceding chapters. Take your sweet time with this. If your time is limited per sitting, come back again and again as time allows, reflecting upon only one of the essentials at each sitting. Be gentle and loving with yourself. Let us begin.

134

Life Purpose

What if the purpose of your life is to find true
peace and love yourself unconditionally?

Self-knowledge comes from asking yourself: "Who am
I in the presence of this, of that, of him, of her?"

Come to love what you do not love
about you. Cease the judgment.
"In the presence of judgment, there is the absence of love."

You must look at your conditioning and belief systems.

Most truths are changeable, relative truths.

You must keep an open mind in order to grow.

The world is as I perceive it to be.
The powerful posture of the **"Perceiver I".**

Learning to know and trust your inner voice

The key to discerning between the voice of your ego and the voice of inner wisdom? *Practice. Practice. Practice.*

Listen   Discern   Decide   Act   Observe

Self-Awareness is critical. Know Yourself.

Have the courage to step out of your comfortable routine.

You want to change your life? Change your life!

Make the commitment.

Observe and follow the flow, the movement.

There are no wrong choices.

There is simply the ideal choice to
achieve the desired outcome.

Reclaiming Peace through Meditation

Peace is who you are at the center of your being.

Peace is a known place, a known state.

Demystifiying meditation. Keep your approach simple.

The purpose of mantra. The power of I AM.

In order to reclaim peace in your human life, you must first bathe yourself in this vibration through meditation.

Practice. Practice. Practice.

Use the meditation download.

Remind yourself frequently: "This is who I AM!"

Where is the Freakin' Joy?

"Joy is a choice you make, not a thing you find."

Emotion is Energy in Motion

We are meant to be the **masters** of our emotions.
Do not deny them but do not indulge in them.

You must be aware of what you are
feeling so that you can choose.

Joy, like Peace, is who you are at the center of your being.

In every moment, with every breath, **Choose Joy!**

The Law of Attraction

The law is immutable and you are already living it.

Like attracts like.

Everything is mostly vibration, energy.

Quantum physics supports and confirms the law of attraction.

Self-Awareness is key. Who am I that manifests?

Feelings, thoughts, words, actions, conditioning, and
beliefs are critical components within the law.

You must attain clarity and maintain
relaxed focus of attention.

You are the great attractor, Master of the Law.

Overcoming Victim Consciousness

You cannot know true peace if you believe that
you are the victim of anyone or anything.

The great and debilitating influence of social consciousness.

Only by taking responsibility for your
life can you change your life.

You influence the collective consciousness and
the collective consciousness influences you.

There is no separation. Quantum physics proves it.

Use the tool of Intent & Outcome

The role of karma and past life actions and attitudes.

You are not a victim.
You are the Master of Your Life!

Sexuality

We are spiritual beings who came here
to live a physical experience.

The physical pleasures, including sexuality,
were meant to be enjoyed.

Enjoyment does not mean addiction.

To know pure love of self you must
cease judging your sexuality.
(Tim's story of accepting his homosexuality)

The negative influence of social and religious conditioning

Sexuality as a great gateway into divine experience
"Oh God!"

Your sexuality is a great tool for rediscovering
love of self and reclaiming personal peace.

Man in the Mirror

The world around me is my mirror.

The world around me reflects to me what I most
need to see about myself in order to know myself
completely and love myself unconditionally.

The "mirror around my neck" exercise

Your teachers are all around you. What
are they "saying" to you?

What are they mirroring to you?

The world around you will mirror to you that which you
do and do not love about you. Be wise. Pay attention!

The best way to change that world is to change yourself.

*"If you want to make the world a better place
Take a look at yourself and make that change."*

The Body Human

Your beautiful body is perhaps your greatest teacher.

The body does not lie.

The "beliefs I have about my body" exercise.

How blocked emotions create disease in the body.

Healing: Aligning with the God Particle within the atom

The play of karma and conscious rebirth

The influence of your environment on the health of your body

Tim's story of healing from pancreatic cancer

The power of Passion for Life

The influence of your everyday thoughts and words on health

The Harvard study on the power of meditation

Conscious Creator Imagery

I am Life! I am Life! I am Life!

The Breath of Life

The Consciousness of One Breath
This place where we are One

You are not alone

Breathing consciously into a healthy
happier more fulfilled life

Transformational Breath Work

Breathing yourself into greater health,
empowerment, clarity and
Unconditional Love

Attachment and the Fear of Death

You cannot know peace if you are
attached to anything or anyone.

When we begin our journey we are
attached to nearly everything.

Detachment is NOT renunciation.
It is not about giving up anything.

The more you love yourself unconditionally, the
less attached you become and vice versa.

Attachment to this human life is your greatest attachment.

Technique: Using that which you love of yourself to let go.

Fear of the unknown fuels the fear of death.
Your life is everlasting.

Enlighten yourself.

Living Your Goodness

The art of acting "as if" or "wearing the coat of"

We are conditioned, programmed, to love what is good.

Wearing the coat of our goodness allows us to become it.

Masters such as Jesus are examples to emulate.

When I act as if I am a loving and giving
person, I feel more love towards myself.

Unconditional love is born out of the conditional.
Use your conditioning to expand the love you are.

Acting "as if" you are good is not lying.
You are already the goodness you seek to become

Ahhhhh. Sweet reflections. You have done very well. Good for you. I have given you much to reflect upon, much to contemplate. I have shared with you pieces of my own story, my own journey. I pray that these will encourage you, inspire you. I reflect upon what I have offered you here and I am pleased—pleased with where I have arrived thus far on my journey, my personal path to true peace and unconditional love of self. These reflections on my part have taught me that, at the age of 64, the journey is far from over. The sharing with you has rejuvenated me, stimulated my passion, my imagining of what is yet to come. The act of sharing with you has strengthened the peace within me and fueled the passion to continue to contribute however I can to the expansion of love and peace in our world. Thank you for being the imagined audience that called this forth from within me.

My dream for you is that you too will one day sit again gazing outward into and upon the life you have lived, the path you have chosen, the long and fruitful journey. As you gaze upon this life a smile breaks upon your beautiful human face, a sigh of contentment, of peace, slips from between your lips. You are pleased with what you view in reflection, the judgments dismissed, the attachments released, the joy attained, the fears conquered, the goodness magnified, the love expanded. At long last. You are pleased with what you can imagine is yet to be created by you. You are pleased. The smile broadens as an awareness of a great truth becomes you:

"I love that I live. I love that I live. I love that I live."

"All that I AM I love. All that I AM I love. All that I AM I love."

"I am Peace. I am Life. I am Love."

So Be it!